ALL THE BEST GAMES
AMAZING FACTS • AWESOME SECRETS

GAME ON! 2016

ⓜSCHOLASTIC

THE WRITERS

ROB ZWETSLOOT

Rob has been writing about games for eight years and can tell you just about anything you would never want to know about *Sonic the Hedgehog*. When he's not trying to convince everyone that Hawlucha is the best Pokémon, Rob dresses up as characters from video games and records really silly videos that seem to make some people laugh.

CHRIS SCULLION

A retro expert who has been gaming since the mid '80s, Chris has regularly contributed to the likes of *Official Nintendo Magazine*, *CVG*, *games™*, and Sky News over the past decade. He'll happily show his boxes full of Japanese Nintendo trinkets to anyone who pretends to care. His amiibo collection is getting a little out of control.

PAUL WALKER-EMIG

Paul started his games journalism career as a freelance writer working for a number of publications before joining the team at NowGamer and then moving into the world of print journalism as a writer for *Play Magazine*. Paul's love of pretentious indie games has earned him a reputation as an insufferable hipster.

ADAM BARNES

Adam's career began by finding collectibles in *Assassin's Creed*, and as a result he's had issues with the series ever since. It must be a fascinating industry to work in, though, because he's still writing about games years later. He's covered wars (console wars, anyway) and all the major gaming conventions, and still finds time to collect trophies and achievements.

REBECCA RICHARDS

Rebecca has been into video games for two decades, and writing about them for around a quarter of that. Her love for games began with *The Illusion of Time* on the SNES, sparking a lifelong addiction to RPGs, stories, puzzles, and adventure s. Her favorite game is *Fez*, although she will also play *Final Fantasy VII* until the comets come home.

VIKKI BLAKE

While some little girls fell in love with TV stars, Vikki fell for video games. She's written for the likes of IGN and Imagine Publishing and firmly believes you don't need l33t skills—or even to know what *l33t* means—to enjoy games. She loves strong stories, authentic characters, and sharing her passion (and extensive retro games collection!) with her son.

DREW SLEEP

Some say Drew found his calling as a games journalist when he got an electric shock from trying to eat an SNES pad when he was four; Drew says he just woke up one morning and "felt like playing video games for a living." No matter how it happened, the games industry is stuck with him now. His favorite game is *Final Fantasy VIII*.

ROSS HAMILTON

Ross spent most of his childhood playing games and writing things, so when it came to looking for work, he realized that writing about games was about the only viable career option he had. He is an average *FIFA* player, an above-average *Hearthstone* player, and firmly of the belief that *Metroid Prime* is the greatest game of all time.

EDITOR
Ryan King

WRITERS
Luke Albigés, Adam Barnes, Vikki Blake, Daniel Cairns, Ross Hamilton, Simon Miller, Rebecca Richards, Chris Scullion, Drew Sleep, Nick Thorpe, Paul Walker-Emig, Josh West, Rob Zwetsloot

LEAD DESIGNER
Andy Downes

DESIGNERS
Lora Barnes, Ali Innes, David Lewis, Steve Mumby, Will Shum, Kym Winters

PRODUCTION
Steve Holmes, Phil King, Amy Squibb

LITTLE-BIGPLANET 3
PLAYSTATION ALL-STARS

LittleBigPlanet 3 has new costumes for the coolest PlayStation characters. Look out for new costumes for Octodad, the casts of *Don't Starve* and *Thomas Was Alone*, and our personal favorite, Lt. Kai Tana from *Velocity 2X*!

STAYING SAFE AND HAVING FUN

Always check out a game's rating before you play it. The ratings are there for a reason, not to keep you from having fun. Here are 10 top tips for staying safe when you're gaming online:

1 Never give out personal information such as your real name or phone number, or anything about your parents.

2 Never agree to meet in person with someone you met online.

3 Remember that any pictures you post might be seen by anyone, and they will be visible for a long time. Don't post pictures that your parents might think aren't appropriate.

4 Tell your parents or a teacher if you come across something that makes you feel uncomfortable

Gaming vloggers are great to watch, but there may be content that's not right for you. Don't watch stuff that obviously isn't made for people your age.

5 Don't respond to any conversations that are mean or make you feel bad. It's not your fault if someone sends you something bad. Let your parents know right away.

6 Talk to your parents about what your family's rules are about how long you can stay online, where you can go, and what you can and can't do.

7 Don't give out your passwords to anyone other than your parents.

8 Don't download or install software to any device or fill out forms without checking with the person who owns the device.

9 When you're online, be nice. Don't say or do anything that could hurt someone else.

10 Games are the most amazing things ever! Let everyone know how to have fun and be safe online

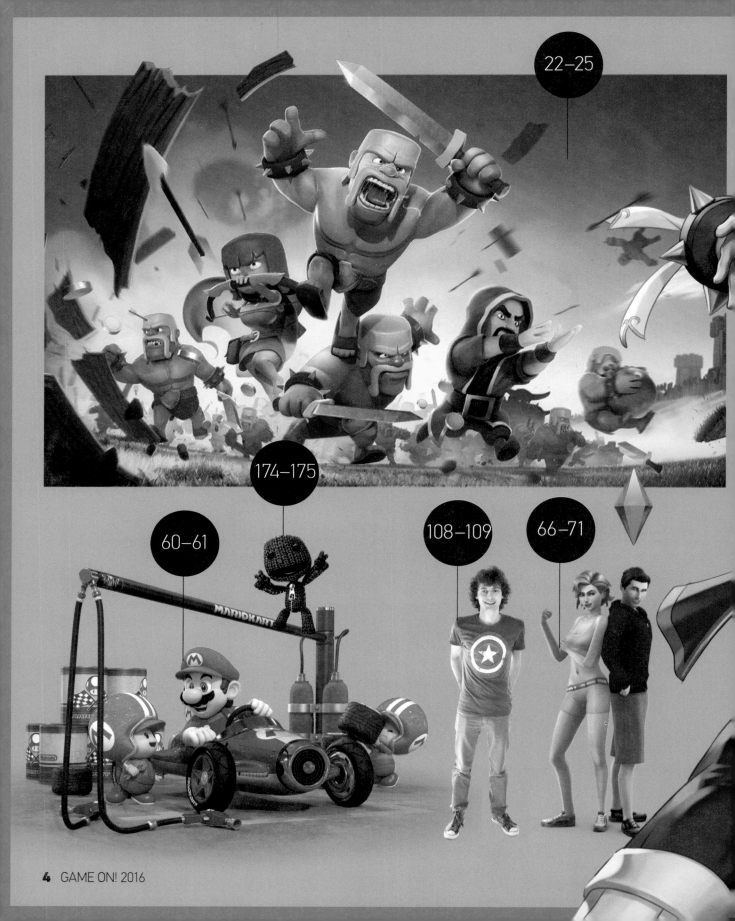

WHAT A YEAR!

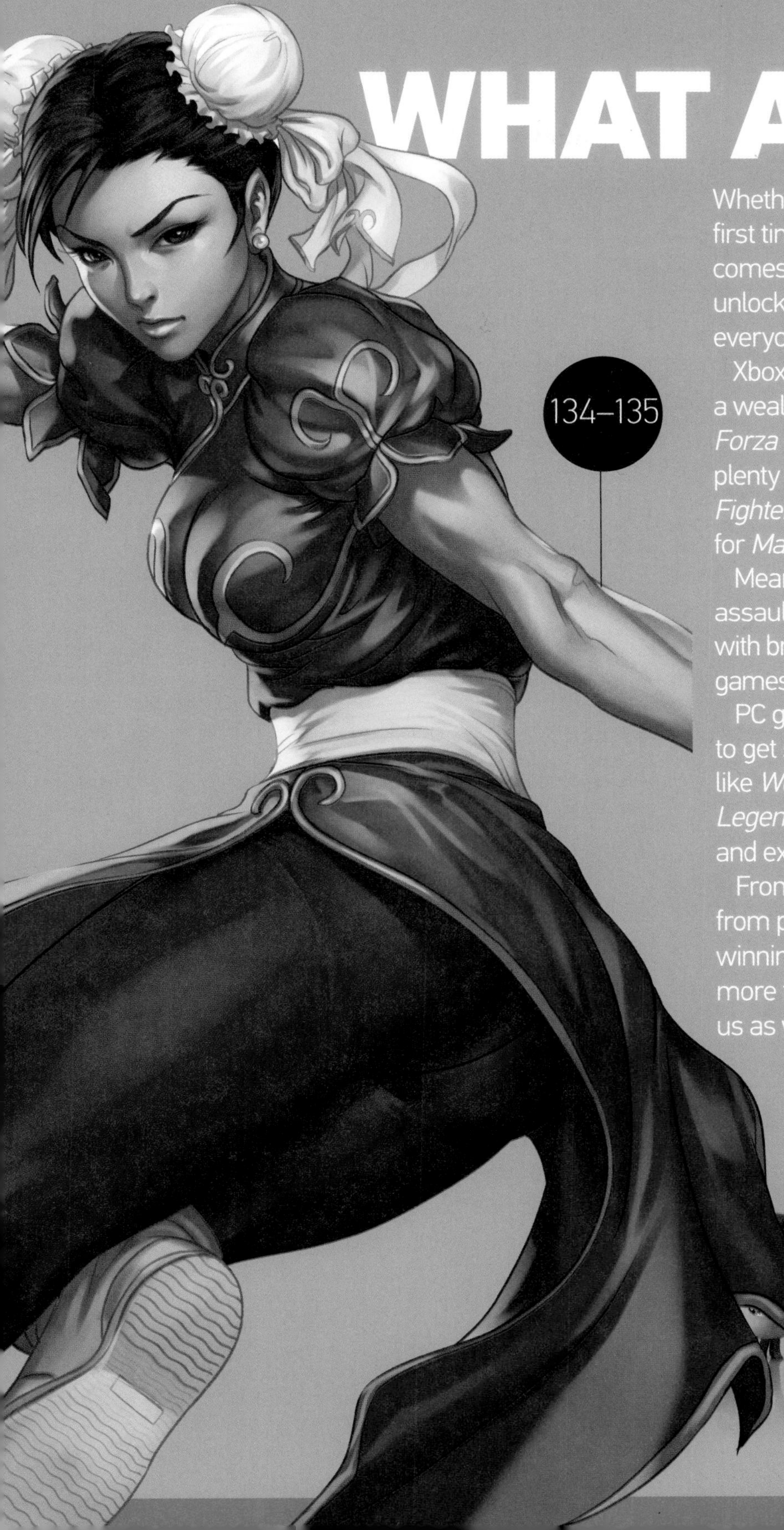

Whether you've just picked up a pad for the first time or you've hit double digits when it comes to the number of platinums you've unlocked, there's been something for everyone in the past 12 months.

Xbox One and PlayStation 4 have seen a wealth of new games released, from *Forza Horizon 2* to *LittleBigPlanet 3*, with plenty more on the way. Excited for *Street Fighter V*? Pumped for *No Man's Sky*? Mad for *Madden*? We've got them all covered.

Meanwhile, Nintendo has continued its assault on friendships around the world with brand-new *Mario Kart* and *Mario Party* games, designed to stoke scorching rivalries.

PC gamers got a new entry in *The Sims* to get sucked into, while old favorites like *World of Warcraft* and *League of Legends* have been refreshed with new and exciting updates.

From conquering cities to exploring space, from powersliding around racetracks to winning the league, our adventures are more fun than you could imagine. So join us as we celebrate gaming!

134–135

76–77

CONTENTS

CONTENTS

LISTS

ROUNDUPS

50 GREATEST GAMING MOMENTS

CLEARING A SET OF BLOCKS IN TETRIS

50 Ah, the simple pleasure of slotting together a set of blocks in the classic *Tetris*. The classic gameplay still lives on today, with *Tetris Ultimate* for Xbox One and PlayStation 4 giving a new generation the chance to get sucked into the quick-fire puzzle game.

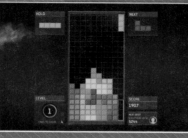

JUMPING ACROSS BUILDINGS IN MIRROR'S EDGE

49 The title that bought parkour to gaming was *Mirror's Edge*. Avoiding conflict by jumping, sliding, and wall running swiftly through the world is not only fun, but different from the action in most other games—it's no surprise that a sequel is on the way!

GETTING ATTACKED BY A MONSTER IN SIMCITY

48 It's terrifying and hilarious the first time you see that Godzilla-like monster wade into the frame to destroy your city. The sublime spectacle is well worth the utter mayhem caused, and thanks to mods, you can do this in the new *SimCity*, too!

REACHING RUBACAVA IN GRIM FANDANGO

47 One of the most satisfying moments in gaming is when Manny becomes a big-shot casino owner . . . and it's a moment we got to relive again, thanks to *Grim Fandango Remastered*!

SONIC ADVENTURE'S KILLER WHALE CHASE

46 Easily the most exciting moment of *Sonic Adventure* is when the blue hedgehog is zipping along Emerald Coast and suddenly a killer whale gives chase—setting the standard for all action moments in current *Sonic* games, on console and mobile alike.

INSULT SWORD FIGHTING IN MONKEY ISLAND

45 En garde! With *The Secret of Monkey Island: Special Edition* now cheaper than ever, you can experience one of the funniest scenes in gaming, as you aim to defeat your opponent with your sharp wit rather than the point of your sword.

GOD OF WAR III'S OPENING

44 One of the most epic opening sequences in gaming sees players dropped straight into the action, climbing up Olympus on the shoulders of a gigantic Titan. Better yet, it doesn't use any CGI, with every detail crafted by the hands of the studio.

OBJECTION, PHOENIX WRIGHT

43 Play the recent *Phoenix Wright: Ace Attorney Trilogy* and you'll notice the attorney's dramatic cry of "Objection," coupled with his famous finger point, highlighting a turning point in the case. It has become such a crucial part of the character that when Phoenix Wright made an appearance in *Ultimate Marvel vs. Capcom 3*, a huge "Objection!" speech bubble was actually one of his special attacks!

A PERFECT RUN IN JET SET RADIO FUTURE

42 Whether it was with the original Dreamcast release or in HD on PlayStation Vita, *Jet Set Radio Future* is a slice of gaming heaven, and little else can match the perfect run, as you pull off sick tricks and spray the city with your neon-colored tags.

YOUR FIRST RAID IN WORLD OF WARCRAFT

41 Do you remember your first raid? Back in 2004, players were trying out the likes of Onyxia's Lair and Molten Core for the first time . . . and over ten years later, there are still new players experiencing their first-ever *World of Warcraft* raids.

SCORING THE WINNING GOAL FROM A DISTANCE IN #IDARB

40 An odd mix of soccer and basketball (with platforming chaos thrown in for good measure), *#IDARB* is one of the best ways to spend time on Xbox One. What we love is how long-range goals are worth more points, leading to blink-and-you'll-miss-it comebacks!

WINNING MASTER LEAGUE IN PES

39 Leading a bunch of nobodies from the depths of the lower leagues to Champions League glory has always been rewarding in *PES*, but that feeling has been amplified by how difficult Master League has become in *PES 2015*.

ORI AND THE BLIND FOREST MAKE US EMOTIONAL . . .

38 The whole game is amazing, but what really stands out is the opening cut scene. We don't want to ruin it for you, because the surprise is part of what makes it so powerful, but if you want proof that stories in games can be moving, *Ori* is all you need.

ESCAPING PRISON IN THE ESCAPISTS

37 Can you find a way to escape from prison? That's what *The Escapists* asks you to do. Whether you do it by stealing keys, digging a tunnel, starting a riot, or using some other devious method, finally tasting freedom is glorious!

PLAYING MINECRAFT ON THE MOVE

36 Of course, fans know that *Minecraft* is already available on smartphone, but honestly, it feels like its real portable home is on Vita. The controls are perfect and the display is gorgeous, plus there are those tricky trophies to unlock . . .

FEELING LONELY IN LIFELESS PLANET

35 You're on your own. That's it! That's the best way to describe this game, which leaves you to explore and figure out exactly why . . . well, we don't want to ruin the mystery! The quiet, creepy atmosphere of this curious game is incredible and has to be experienced.

THE MUSIC LEVELS IN RAYMAN LEGENDS

34 A brilliant marriage of music and gameplay, *Rayman Legends* has you timing your jumps to the song being played as you run through the stage at breakneck speed. Barreling along to the game's quirky renditions of "Eye of the Tiger," "Woo Hoo," and our personal fave, "Black Betty," is sure to put a smile on your face.

PLAYING GOLDENEYE MULTIPLAYER

33 One of the best multiplayer experiences you can have is four-player split screen in *GoldenEye* on the N64. For a mode that the studio admitted was added as a "complete afterthought," it was incredible fun, and it kick-started the idea of FPS multiplayer on console.

CRAFTING A LEVEL IN LITTLEBIGPLANET 3

32 Usually, the game developers make the games and we play them. *LittleBigPlanet* changed all that, by giving us the tools to create our own levels and share them with the world. What's amazing is developer Media Molecule didn't think players would take to the creative side of *LittleBigPlanet*, and it was only when Sony gave the studio its full backing that the team had the confidence and drive to create the experience we all know and love today!

SPOILER ALERT! A SURPRISE AWAITS IN STAR WARS: KNIGHTS OF THE OLD REPUBLIC

31 It's one of the best RPGs ever made, with one of the most surprising twists we've ever seen . . . and it's recently been rereleased on iPad and Android!

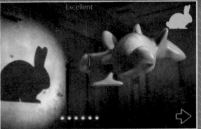

CREATING FUNKY SHAPES WITH SHADOWMATIC

30 This puzzle game is one of the most relaxing you'll ever play, as you create shapes with shadows using the objects given to you. It's easy to understand and easier to play, and you can create hilarious shapes while trying to find the right answer!

PLAYING ROCK BAND 3 WITH A FULL BAND

29 Rocking out to your fave tunes with a *Rock Band* guitar has always been great fun, but the game is at its absolute best when your friends are manning the other instruments and jamming along with you. With *Rock Band 4* on the way, this is the best way to get warmed up!

EXPERIENCING THE MAYHEM OF GOAT SIMULATOR MMO

28 As if *Goat Simulator* wasn't already crazy enough, the insanity was increased tenfold with *Goat Simulator MMO*. There aren't even words to describe just how chaotic this game is— it's a unique form of ridiculous mayhem!

WITNESSING THE POWER OF NATURE IN CITIES: SKYLINES

27 Flooding your own city is more of a "whoops!" moment than something that stands as one of gaming's greatest . . . but the game's attention to detail forces you to plan and really think about what you're doing. Plus, it's an awesome sight to behold!

THE MASTER ONION RAP IN PARAPPA THE RAPPER

23 The most memorable song from the game that introduced rhythm action to the West has to be *PaRappa the Rapper*'s first tune. "Kick, punch, it's all in the mind . . ." You can pick up the original classic on PS Vita and get lost in the funky rhythms all over again!

RELIVING LEMMINGS MEMORIES WITH FLOCKERS

26 Remember *Lemmings*? The puzzle game that saw you herding the little creatures past obstacles to the exit? *Flockers* is the modern take on that classic. Sheep replace the lemmings, but it's still the same mix of tricky levels and deadly traps!

RUNNING A FAST BREAK IN NBA 2K15

22 There's no greater joy in *NBA 2K15* than grabbing a rebound from your opponent's missed shot, quickly throwing a pass up the court, and sprinting away for a monstrous slam-dunk finish. It's an intense feeling, and you'll definitely punch the air when you first pull this off!

SCORING A SCREAMER IN FIFA

25 Just as seeing your favorite soccer team score a goal never gets old, you'll never get tired of smashing a shot from 30 yards and seeing it fly into the top corner. Hitting the back of the net is always great, no matter how you do it, but this is a special feeling.

BEATING YOUR FRIENDS' SCORES IN TRIALS HD

21 *Trials HD* and the more recent *Trials Fusion* are responsible for creating scorching-hot high-score rivalries among friends. And to think, this from a series that started as a mere flash game!

DOING A COMBO THROUGH THE ENTIRE LEVEL IN OLLIOLLI 2

24 The great thing about *OlliOlli 2* is how you learn it in stages. First you get through the level. Then you string together some simple combos. Then you get ambitious and try to complete the level in a single combo. The satisfying feeling when you do so is immense!

FIGHTING A DRAGON IN NEVERWINTER NIGHTS

20 Being the first MMO on Xbox One makes *Neverwinter Nights* interesting enough ... but level up enough and you can take part in some truly major battles that stand out in the MMO genre, such as the fierce battle against this deadly dragon!

THROWING A HUGE TOUCHDOWN PASS IN MADDEN NFL 15

19 Few things beat the feeling you get when you sling a last-second Hail Mary pass down the field in *Madden NFL* and see your receiver somehow catch the ball and take off. What makes this feeling extra sweet is knowing how annoyed your opponent will be!

SMASHING A HIGH SCORE IN TONY HAWK'S 3

18 The revert was the key to high scores in *Tony Hawk's 3*, opening up exciting combo possibilities. The move was so important and added so much creativity to the gameplay that Activision released the *Tony Hawk's 3* revert as DLC for *Tony Hawk's Pro Skater HD*!

PLAYING BROKEN AGE, THE FIRST TRUE KICKSTARTER SUCCESS

17 Point-and-click adventure *Broken Age* was a huge landmark for the games industry, since it was the game that put Kickstarter on the map and proved that crowd-funded projects could thrive. It also helped that *Broken Age* was just so much fun to play through!

FINISHING SHOVEL KNIGHT

16 Not only do we recommend *Shovel Knight* for all PC, PS4, and Xbox One owners, it's also one of the hardest games ever made! Completing it is a big accomplishment, and it's worth persisting just for the immense sense of satisfaction you'll get.

FLOPPING AROUND AS A . . . PIECE OF BREAD?!

15 It might not be the best game you'll ever play, but it will definitely be one of the weirdest! Those first awkward moments in *I Am Bread*, when you're trying to flop around the kitchen, are the only time clumsy controls in any game will have you howling with laughter.

ESTABLISHING CONTACT IN CIVILIZATION: BEYOND EARTH

14 One of the new ways to win in *Civilization: Beyond Earth*, which sets the strategic fun in space, is to establish contact with an advanced alien race. How many games let you do that? It's fantastic for those who don't want to rely on the usual method of military might.

WINNING A RACE IN MARIO KART

13 Let's face it, winning is fun. Combine the greatest kart-racing series of all time with the satisfaction of crossing the finish line first and you've got yourself a winning formula. It doesn't matter which entry in the *Mario Kart* series you're playing, beating the competition is always awesome, particularly if you're racing friends. Victory is extra delicious if you can take your first-place buddy out with a green shell right on the finish line to steal a win.

CONQUERING MONUMENT VALLEY AND FEELING SMART

12 Almost every game on this list tests your skill and your reactions. Not *Monument Valley*, which is a test of how smart you are and whether you can see through the optical illusions it uses to try to lead you astray. Beat this game and you'll feel like a genius!

SLIDING DOWN THE SLOPE IN JOURNEY

10 You're gliding freely down a slope in the middle of a vast desert and you see the Sun setting, low on the horizon. It breaks through the arches of a ruin to light up the sand with an amazing golden glow. It's a beautiful moment in the video game *Journey*.

GAZING AT EVERY CURVE AND DETAIL IN PROJECT CARS

11 Games look better and better all the time, as developers figure out tricks to squeeze every last drop of visual power from the consoles they're working on. Has any car in any game looked quite as stunning as those in *Project CARS*? Our open jaws think not!

PULLING THE SWORD FROM THE STONE IN OCARINA OF TIME

9 When you pull the Master Sword from the stone, you realize you've been tricked by Ganondorf in a brilliant twist, frozen for years while he takes over the kingdom. When you're brought out of limbo, you're all grown up— and now you're energized to take off and save the world!

GETTING PAST THE FIRST WORLD IN SPELUNKY

8 One of the things we all love about games is the challenge. At times, *Spelunky* tested our patience on that front— it's one of the most difficult games you can play. However, that just makes your fist pump bigger when you finally get past *Spelunky*'s first world!

TACKLING THE FIRST BOSS IN SHADOW OF THE COLOSSUS

7 One of the reasons *Shadow of the Colossus* is one of the best games of all time, and remains so with its HD rerelease on PS3, is because of its mountainous bosses. That moment when you saw the first monster towering above you was incredible and humbling.

DOING A HADOUKEN IN ULTRA STREET FIGHTER IV

6 *Street Fighter* has one of the most famous special moves of all time: Ryu's hadouken. It's an iconic move, and one of the most important in the game, since it shows that you can be just as effective from a safe distance as you can be up close with your fists and feet!

THE OPENING SCENE IN FINAL FANTASY X

5 Thanks to the recent HD rerelease on PS3, PS4, and PS Vita, we get to experience the delicate beauty of this scene all over again. The party's weapons are cast to the ground, they're all quietly sitting around a fire, and "Back to Zanarkand" plays on a lonely piano. Absolutely gorgeous.

PULLING OFF A DRAMATIC HEARTHSTONE COMEBACK

4 There's no such thing as an easy battle in tense, dramatic, strategic *Hearthstone*... You have to consider the cards you have, the cards your opponent has, and the way they like to play, and adjust your tactics accordingly. But nothing will make you triumphantly punch the air like snatching victory from the jaws of defeat with clever moves that surprise your opponent, considering how difficult it is to skillfully orchestrate a comeback!

CHOOSING YOUR FIRST POKEMON

3 You collect many Pokémon throughout the course of a *Pokémon* game, but somehow there's never one that means as much as that very first partner Pokémon. It doesn't matter whether your first *Pokémon* game was *Pokémon Red Version* or *Pokémon Blue Version* back on the Game Boy, or more recently *Pokémon X* or *Pokémon Y* on Nintendo 3DS—you'll never forget the first Pokémon you chose. That Pokémon felt like "yours" more than any other after the two of you grew and become more powerful together, paired up on your quest to defeat every Gym Leader.

TOP **5** LEGO GAMES

STAR WARS COMPLETE SAGA

1 *Star Wars* has long been acquainted with LEGO, with real-life LEGO sets based on the film series. I's even more fun in video-game form, as you take control of Jedi, robots and strange aliens!

LEGO BATMAN

2 Everyone loves playing as superheroes, and Batman is one of the most popular of the bunch. Even better, however, is how this *LEGO* game lets you play as a wide range of heroes and villains.

LEGO INDIANA JONES

3 Indiana Jones is a guy all about having exciting adventures in places only our imaginations could dream up, so it makes sense that he should be turned into a video game.

LEGO HARRY POTTER YEARS 1–4

4 The addition of magic makes LEGO even more fun. Plus, it's impossible not to laugh when you see Hogwarts, Harry and his friends, and all the events of the films built in LEGO bricks!

LEGO MARVEL SUPER HEROES

5 One of the more recent *LEGO* games, this one is the most impressive, letting you explore a LEGO version of New York.

TIME LINE

1997 – LEGO ISLAND
1998 – LEGO CREATOR
2001 – BIONICLE: THE GAME
2002 – LEGO SOCCER MANIA
2004 – LEGO KNIGHTS' KINGDOM
2006 – BIONICLE: HEROES
2007 – LEGO STAR WARS: THE COMPLETE SAGA
2008 – LEGO BATMAN: THE VIDEOGAME
2007 – LEGO INDIANA JONES: THE ORIGINAL ADVENTURES
2009 – LEGO BATTLES
2009 – LEGO ROCK BAND
2010 – LEGO HARRY POTTER YEARS 1–4
2011 – LEGO STAR WARS III: THE CLONE WARS
2011 – LEGO CREATIONARY
2013 – LEGO FRIENDS
2013 – LEGO CITY UNDERCOVER
2014 – LEGO: THE HOBBIT
2014 – THE LEGO MOVIE GAME
2015 – MARVEL'S AVENGERS
2015 – LEGO JURASSIC WORLD

ALSO CHECK OUT . . .

LEGO MINIFIGURES
Taking the idea of minifigures to a whole new level, *LEGO Minifigures* is a huge online game that lets you explore famous LEGO sets.

LEGO JURASSIC WORLD
The latest *LEGO* adventure focuses on the blockbuster movies, and you can even build your own dinosaurs!

LEGO DIGITAL DESIGNER
It isn't exactly a game—it's software that gives you access to an infinite number of LEGO bricks!

TOP 10 STUNNING VISUALS

DID YOU KNOW?

Princess Peach wasn't originally a playable character in *Super Mario 3D World*. She was included last minute to add an extra competitive edge.

MARIO KART 8

WHY: The first to be developed in HD, the long-running racing title looks absolutely stunning on the Wii U, with everything from the karts to each course looking like it's been brought to life. The originality of each track helped, too, with environments ranging from icy mountains to lush forests.

KNACK

WHY: Launching alongside the PS4, *Knack* was long built up as an example of how powerful Sony's new console was going to be. Thankfully, it lived up to all the hype. *Knack* looked so good in motion that you could easily forgive someone for thinking it was an animated movie, with its incredible, larger-than-life characters.

CHILD OF LIGHT

WHY: *Child of Light* doesn't look like most other games—it looks better. Every aspect of *Child of Light*, from the main character to each level, stands out to such a degree that you'll forget you're supposed to be playing the thing—you'll be too busy just staring at the high standard of visual sheen.

DONKEY KONG: TROPICAL FREEZE

WHY: Whether you're caught in a storm, swimming underwater, exploring a saw mill, or trying to punch an octopus, this is one of the Wii U's most stunning games, and deliberately so. It's a technical showpiece.

FORZA HORIZON 2

WHY: Most racing games try to show off the grunt of a console, and *Forza Horizon 2* is no different. One of the Xbox One's most attractive offerings, it absolutely lives up to what people expected from a new generation of consoles.

RAYMAN LEGENDS

WHY: *Rayman Legends* creator Michel Ancel wanted his game to look a little different. So he made sure that every character, level, item, weapon, and boss was drawn from scratch. The result is something very special, and *Rayman Legends* is one of the best-looking games of all time.

GRIM FANDANGO REMASTERED

WHY: *Grim Fandango* was always a good-looking game, but because it came out well over ten years ago, it has aged considerably. Thanks to Sony and its PS4, however, *Grim Fandango* has been remastered for a whole new era, meaning that you can enjoy one of the best point-and-click games ever made and not be put off by its visuals.

THE LEGEND OF ZELDA: THE WIND WAKER

WHY: The prettiest *Zelda* game of them all, *Wind Waker* made people stand up and take notice. With its cel-shaded art style, it became even more attractive when it was rereleased for the Wii U in HD. While many games try to look as lifelike as possible, *Zelda* had a formula of its own.

SHADOW OF THE COLOSSUS HD

WHY: Nothing about *Shadow of the Colossus* was ordinary, including the impressive visuals. Creating a faraway land, Team ICO did an amazing job at making sure you felt alone by inserting sweeping deserts and distant horizons into the mix. On top of this, coming face-to-face with one of the game's mammoth beasts was awe inspiring.

CASTLE OF ILLUSION STARRING MICKEY MOUSE

WHY: Do you remember *Castle of Illusion* on the Mega Drive? Possibly not. Well, when it was released, most people agreed that it was one of the best-looking games around, and Sega kindly rereleased it back in 2013.

THE EXPERT SAYS . . .
MATTHEW FREEMAN
"SplatterCatGaming" on YouTube

FINAL FANTASY TACTICS

The most aesthetically pleasing game ever made is a tough one for me, because I lean heavily in favor of animation. I'd say it's probably *Final Fantasy Tactics* for me personally. I loved that period of game development when 2-D sprites were set on blocky 3-D backgrounds. Mode 7 is fairly representative of my childhood and the way I view gaming in my head. *Dust: An Elysian Tale* is also insanely gorgeous to look at.

TOP 10 BIGGEST GAME WORLDS

FUEL

WHY: This open-world racer's world is absolutely huge, clocking in at a mammoth 5,400 square miles. That's roughly the size of Connecticut! You can also drive wherever you want without any loading screens, which makes the monstrous racer feel even bigger. You don't have to race, either, with the option to free roam.

MINECRAFT

WHY: The randomly generated world isn't quite infinite, but it certainly feels like it is, and the beauty of *Minecraft* is that you don't even need to venture off as far as the eye can see. You can carve out your own pocket of the world and call it yours. But it's nice to know the option for exploration is there, should you get itchy feet!

EVE ONLINE

WHY: We could put ten different MMORPGs on this list, but if we had to be picky, of course we're going to choose one set in space! With thousands of solar systems to explore, and "wormhole space" systems to discover as well, there's plenty here to get sucked into. Good luck finding it all!

DARK SOULS

WHY: In terms of raw size, *Dark Souls* can't compare to the other games on this list. So why feature it at all? Because no other game forces players to cover every inch of ground like *Dark Souls* does, and as a result, it feels like the biggest game ever. It can take days to make just feet of progress!

ELDER SCROLLS: SKYRIM

WHY: The *Elder Scrolls* series has always believed that bigger is better—*Daggerfall*, for instance, had seemingly endless borders. But *Skyrim* combines a huge world with intricate detail. It feels real, it feels alive, and there's almost no filler.

JUST CAUSE 2

WHY: It's known nowadays for its crazy physics and insane stunts, but *Just Cause 2* is also an absolutely enormous game, with the fictional island of Panau clocking in at around 400 square miles. That's a lot of island to explore . . .

BURNOUT PARADISE

WHY: *Test Drive Unlimited* might take the sim-racing crown in a size contest, but its arcade rival *Burnout Paradise* packed in the extras across its vast expanse, from billboards for smashing through to smart shortcuts that allowed you to take daring and exciting new routes. So just how big is *Burnout Paradise*? Incredibly, its world is double the size of the map in *Grand Theft Auto: San Andreas*!

TEST DRIVE UNLIMITED

WHY: This open-world racer was loosely modeled after satellite images taken of the Hawaiian island of Oahu. Although some notable landmarks were missing, the team managed to re-create about 1,000 miles of road and highway to drive on! *Test Drive Unlimited* was a fun racing game, plus it was so vast that it felt just as enjoyable as a virtual tourist simulator, allowing you to drive around and take in the sights!

NO MAN'S SKY

WHY: The lofty claim for *No Man's Sky* is that it would take a staggering 5 billion years to visit every single planet in its universe, even if you were exploring those planets for just a single second each. Incredible! We're pretty confident in saying that you're not going to see everything this huge exploration adventure has to offer, regardless of how dedicated to the cause of exploring you might be . . .

OPERATION FLASHPOINT: DRAGON RISING

WHY: Based directly on the Alaskan island of Kiska, the world of *Dragon Rising* stretches across miles of land with towns, lakes, forests, and volcanic terrain. In an unusual move for an FPS, missions begin nowhere near the final objective, forcing a long-haul trek toward the action.

WHAT ABOUT THE SMALLEST GAMES EVER?

THE ROOM 2

So you know what the biggest games ever made are. What about the smallest games? They almost all belong to the "escape the room" genre, in which you're stuck in a single room and you have to pick up items and use your brain to figure out how to leave.

The biggest success in the genre is *The Room* and its recent sequel, *The Room 2*. They're incredibly hard games to complete, but what makes them so special is that you have unlimited time to solve them, and you can call on the community for advice.

You can also find examples as free-to-play Internet games, with Japanese developers making a large number of them. Fortunately, they rarely use any text, so language barriers aren't a problem—check out the tricky *Escraft* by 58 WORKS if you want a real challenge to sink your teeth into!

STREET FIGHTER

ROUND ONE . . . FIGHT!

There's no arguing with it: *Street Fighter* is the world's most popular beat-'em-up game. Now well over 25 years old, the series gained a fresh new audience with *Street Fighter IV*'s Ultra attacks, Focus moves, and new characters such as Rufus and El Fuerte, becoming one of the biggest competitive games in the world! The latest update, *Ultra Street Fighter IV*, rebalances the existing cast and adds some new faces such as acrobatic Rolento and dominant Hugo.

With *Street Fighter IV* drawing to a close, Capcom has announced *Street Fighter V*, which will feature a brand-new combo system and stunning new graphics. The bad news: It's not out until 2016. We simply cannot wait to get our hands on it!

DID YOU KNOW?

Balrog was called M. Bison in Japan, as he looked Mike Tyson. In the US, Balrog and M. Bison had their names swapped to avoid legal action!

STATS

Street Fighter IV has an average score of

94
on Metacritic

£260
million:

the amount that *Street Fighter II* arcade machines in the UK took in in one year

There are over

80
games in the entire *Street Fighter* franchise

There have been

90

playable characters across all *Street Fighter* games

TOP **5** CHARACTERS

RYU

1 The most iconic of all of the Street Fighters and one of the most recognizable characters in gaming, Ryu is easy to pick up but hard to master, and has appeared in every *Street Fighter* game to date. In some games he is playable as Evil Ryu, the version of his character that would exist if he had murderous ideas.

KEN

2 Boasting many of the same moves as Ryu, and taking the spot as his best friend despite their rivalry, Ken is among the more brash and arrogant characters in *Street Fighter*. He's loved and hated by players in equal measure, given that he's very accessible for beginners. Like Ryu, Ken appears in every game.

GUILE

3 The all-American tough guy has been a mainstay of the series for years and is well known for being a hard character to perfect. In the game, he was originally an army major, avenging the death of one of his buddies at the hands of M. Bison. "Guile's Theme" has also become a sensation on YouTube.

CHUN-LI

4 The first and only female character in *Street Fighter II*, Chun-Li has become synonymous with the *Street Fighter* series. She paved the way for more female characters in beat-'em-up games and is now one of the most recognizable individuals in the entire world of gaming.

M. BISON

5 The long-running bad guy of the *Street Fighter* story, M. Bison wasn't always a playable character. This was eventually changed, and the leader of the Shadaloo crime syndicate is now one of the most beloved combatants in Capcom's series. Many characters have vendettas against this evil overlord.

TIME LINE

1987 – STREET FIGHTER

1990 – STREET FIGHTER 2010: THE FINAL FIGHT

1992 – STREET FIGHTER II': CHAMPION EDITION

1992 – STREET FIGHTER II TURBO

1995 – STREET FIGHTER ALPHA

1996 – STREET FIGHTER EX

1996 – X-MEN VS. STREET FIGHTER

1997 – STREET FIGHTER III: NEW GENERATION

1997 – MARVEL SUPER HEROES VS. STREET FIGHTER

1998 – SUPER STREET ALPHA 3

1998 – STREET FIGHTER EX2

2000 – MARVEL VS. CAPCOM 2: NEW AGE OF HEROES

2000 – STREET FIGHTER EX3

2004 – HYPER STREET FIGHTER II: THE ANNIVERSARY EDITION

2008 – STREET FIGHTER IV

2010 – SUPER STREET FIGHTER IV

2011 – MARVEL VS. CAPCOM 3: FATE OF TWO WORLDS

2012 – STREET FIGHTER X TEKKEN

2014 – ULTRA STREET FIGHTER IV

ALSO CHECK OUT . . .

TEKKEN 6
One of the longest running beat-'em-ups in video-game history, *Tekken* had a crossover with *Street Fighter*, released in 2012.

SUPER SMASH BROS.
Featuring all your favorite Nintendo characters, *Super Smash Bros.* is so simple that anyone can play it.

SOUL CALIBUR V
A weapon-based fighting game, *Soul Calibur* involves precise gameplay and a varied cast of characters, such as the eccentric Voldo!

VELOCITY 2X

SAVE THE GALAXY

How fast are your reactions? That's a question *Velocity 2X* asks you, millions of times per second, on an endless loop. It takes old-school twitch-shooter gameplay and updates it with gorgeous modern visuals. Strap yourself in and hang on!

SUPER SMASH BROS.

HAVE A SMASHING TIME!

Super Smash Bros. is a dream come true for a lot of people. Taking Nintendo's (and other developers') biggest characters and allowing them to duke it out in the same arena, it gave gamers the chance to see the likes of Pikachu vs. Link, Pac-Man vs. Kirby, and, of course, the score-settling Mario vs. Sonic. The crossover combat continued with *Super Smash Bros.* on 3DS and Wii U, which hit the shelves last year and continued the excellence the series has been known for. A whole host of new characters was brought in, from Rosalina to Dark Pit, and online play meant you could challenge anyone in the world, with For Fun and For Glory modes separating the casual fighters from the hard-core professionals!

DID YOU KNOW?

Super Smash Bros. was originally called *Dragon King: The Fighting Game* and featured no Nintendo characters. They were added for "atmosphere."

STATS

Average score of
92
on Metacritic for *Super Smash Bros. Wii U*

49.
number of characters in *Super Smash Bros. Wii U* at release

1
million: copies of *Super Smash Bros. 3DS* sold in the first week

1999.
the year the first *Super Smash Bros.* came out

TOP **5** BEST BEGINNER CHARACTERS

MARIO

1 Mario is one of the best-known faces in gaming, and therefore one of the easiest to use in *Smash Bros.* Use his fiery projectile attack to keep opponents at bay and his cape to deflect enemy fire.

VILLAGER

2 Straight from the streets of *Animal Crossing*, the versatile Villager character can catch other people's projectiles to use them later in the fight. When he does, they're even more powerful than they were before.

DUCK HUNT

3 On paper, Duck Hunt looks complicated, but thanks to good move recovery, great aerial attacks, three different projectiles, and a solid level of speed, the Dog and the Duck are great characters to hold your own with.

LINK

4 If you become really good at *Super Smash Bros.*, Link becomes a character with a lot of depth. When you first start out with Link, his numerous projectile attacks mean that you can hold off most opponents with relative ease. He has appeared in all *Super Smash Bros.* games and is a clear favorite.

LITTLE MAC

5 From the *Punch-Out!!* series comes Little Mac. Unlike the rest of the characters here, Little Mac doesn't have any projectile attacks. He is, however, excellent at defending against them. So if you would rather get up close and personal with *Smash Bros.*, Mac is the character for you.

TIME LINE

Year	Title
1999	SUPER SMASH BROS.
2001	SUPER SMASH BROS. MELEE
2008	SUPER SMASH BROS. BRAWL
2014	SUPER SMASH BROS. 3DS
2014	SUPER SMASH BROS. WII U

ALSO CHECK OUT . . .

PLAYSTATION ALL-STARS BATTLE ROYALE
It's nowhere near as good as *Smash Bros.*, but if you're more of a Sony fan, this will satisfy that smashing urge.

SMALL ARMS
Available on Xbox Live Arcade, *Small Arms* is a low-budget *Smash Bros.*, designed to offer half the features for half the price. It's entertaining enough.

TEENAGE MUTANT NINJA TURTLES: SMASH-UP
Released on Wii U, *Smash-Up* does a fair job of re-creating the *Smash Bros.* format, as long as you're a TMNT fan.

BATMAN: ARKHAM

BIOGRAPHY

It's hard to deny that Batman is the coolest superhero around. With his skills in hand-to-hand combat, his supersharp intelligence, and all those gadgets, Batman has it all. So if players want to imagine that they *are* Batman, there's no better way than with the *Arkham* series of games—which show off every aspect of the famed hero. The upcoming *Batman: Arkham Knight*, which will be rated Mature, may make players feel even cooler while playing as the caped crusader, with Batarang sensors they can throw out to gain intel, and grapple guns that can be fired midflight to chain awesome gliding moves together. And players will finally get to race around in the Batmobile—a dream come true for almost every Batman fan out there!

DID YOU KNOW?

Developer Rocksteady hid a secret in the original *Arkham Asylum* game that teased details about the sequel, *Arkham City.*

STATS

Batman: Arkham City has an average score of

96
on Metacritic

13
different Bat-gadgets are used throughout the *Arkham* games

6
games are included in the series

The series has featured

58
characters from the *Batman* comics

TOP **5** BAT-GADGETS

CAPE

1 Anyone who has played the *Arkham* series will understand why the cape is ranked first. Whether you're flying through Arkham Asylum or soaring above Arkham City, taking to the skies is incredibly fun. There will be a bunch of new aerial moves in *Arkham Knight* for players to choose from.

BATCLAW

2 As the primary means of reaching higher points, the Batclaw is perhaps the most often used gadget in the *Arkham* games, but it's particularly fun to use on an enemy in the middle of a fight if you get the angle and timing just right. The reward? A big old Batboot right in the enemy's face!

SHOCK GLOVES

3 These aren't technically Batman's gadgets, but he does acquire them from the Electrocutioner in *Arkham Origins*. They give his punches even more devastating power—as if being hit by Batman wasn't bad enough!

EXPLOSIVE GEL

4 When the enemies are equipped with rifles, there isn't much Batman's fists can do— that's where his explosive gel comes in! The Predator sections of the *Arkham* games are easier if players learn how to make good use of this gadget.

BATMOBILE

5 The Batmobile is playable exclusively in *Batman: Arkham Knight*, but it's recognizable to all Batman fans. It's basically a tank for dispersing large groups of enemies, plus it can also act as a superfast vehicle that can even drive on walls!

TIME LINE

2009 – BATMAN: ARKHAM ASYLUM

2011 – BATMAN: ARKHAM CITY

2011 – BATMAN: ARKHAM CITY LOCKDOWN

2013 – BATMAN: ARKHAM ORIGINS BLACKGATE

2013 – BATMAN: ARKHAM ORIGINS

2015 – BATMAN: ARKHAM KNIGHT

ALSO CHECK OUT . . .

CAPTAIN AMERICA: SUPER SOLDIER
The combat system is almost exactly the same as in the *Arkham* games, so it's worth giving this a try!

SPIDER-MAN SHATTERED DIMENSIONS
Spider-Man may be on the other side of the superhero fence, but he's a great hero all the same. This game proves it.

INFAMOUS: SECOND SON
Superhero games usually focus on characters from existing comics or films, but the powers in *InFamous* are just as fun as any known hero's.

SUPERHERO ROUNDUP

GET YOUR CAPE ON . . .

Superheroes can be the perfect video-game characters. They're all about exciting battles and special powers—saving the world and doing so in style. There's been plenty of superhero action keeping gamers busy in the past year, too. The DC-flavored *Infinite Crisis* MOBA continues to grow with new characters, and *DC Universe Online* players now have the Munitions superpower to play around with, adding more variety to an already huge game. There has also been superhero fun on mobile devices, thanks to *X-Men: Mutant Mayhem* and *Guardians of the Galaxy: The Universal Weapon*.

It hasn't all been serious, brooding business, though, with *LEGO Batman 3: Beyond Gotham* providing a smaller take on the classic characters we all know and love!

DID YOU KNOW?

Since 1982, Marvel has released at least one video game every year, except for 1983, 1988, and 1998. The most it released in one year was ten in 2011.

STATS

Comics:

6.85 million copies
of the *InFamous* series have been bought worldwide

9: Marvel creator Stan Lee has had cameos in nine different games

Video games:

135 different games
based on Marvel comics

74 games
based on DC comics

TOP **5** SUPERHERO GAMES

MARVEL: ULTIMATE ALLIANCE (2006)

1 This neat co-op action RPG let you pick your favorite Marvel character and battle villains alongside your friends.

INFAMOUS SECOND SON (2014)

2 This third entry in the series was one of the few not based on existing superheroes. Graphics geeks can get excited at the amazing particle effects, which push the PlayStation 4 as far as it will go!

SPIDER-MAN 2 (2004)

3 *Spider-Man 2* remains one of the best superhero games, if only for its ability to give you complete freedom—as Spidey himself—to websling your way around a virtual version of New York. It's been improved on since but still remains a classic.

DID YOU KNOW?

Super Mario 64's boo ghosts were based on the assistant director's wife, who was angry about the time he spent at work!

LEGO MARVEL SUPER HEROES (2013)

4 Similar to *Spider-Man 2*, the recent *LEGO Marvel Super Heroes* lets you explore New York however you choose. Being able to pick from a huge roster of characters is what makes it great.

X-MEN ARCADE (1992)

5 This one is so old, it first appeared in the arcades. It was a side-scrolling beat-'em-up in which you could play as one of six memorable X-Men—Wolverine, Cyclops, Colossus, Storm, Dazzler, or Nightcrawler.

TIME LINE

Year	Title
1988	SUPERMAN
1994	THE DEATH AND RETURN OF SUPERMAN
1995	MARVEL SUPER HEROES
1997	SPAWN: THE ETERNAL
1998	MARVEL VS. CAPCOM: CLASH OF SUPER HEROES
1999	SPAWN: IN THE DEMON'S HAND
1999	SUPERMAN
2000	MARVEL VS. CAPCOM 2: NEW AGE OF HEROES
2002	FREEDOM FORCE
2002	SPIDER-MAN
2003	SPAWN: ARMAGEDDON
2003	VIEWTIFUL JOE
2004	CITY OF HEROES
2004	SPIDER-MAN 2
2005	THE INCREDIBLE HULK: ULTIMATE DESTRUCTION
2005	ULTIMATE SPIDER-MAN
2006	JUSTICE LEAGUE HEROES
2006	MARVEL ULTIMATE ALLIANCE
2007	SPIDER-MAN 3
2008	THE INCREDIBLE HULK
2008	MORTAL KOMBAT VS. DC UNIVERSE
2009	INFAMOUS
2009	PROTOTYPE
2009	MARVEL ULTIMATE ALLIANCE 2
2009	CHAMPIONS ONLINE
2010	COMIC JUMPER
2011	INFAMOUS 2
2011	MARVEL VS CAPCOM 3: FATE OF TWO WORLDS
2011	DC UNIVERSE ONLINE
2011	CAPTAIN AMERICA: SUPER SOLDIER
2012	PROTOTYPE 2
2013	INJUSTICE GODS AMONG US
2013	MARVEL HEROES
2013	THE WONDERFUL 101
2014	INFAMOUS SECOND SON
2014	INFAMOUS FIRST LIGHT

![50 HARDEST ACHIEVEMENTS & TROPHIES (AND HOW TO UNLOCK THEM)]

THE CREW
THE EXTRA MILE

1 When you hit level 50, you'll unlock the ability to earn platinum medals. Once you have platinum medals on all levels, the Extra Mile is unlocked. That's really difficult—we'd suggest owning cars across all five specs at level 1200+ before trying. We recommend Mini Cooper S, Ford Focus RS, Hummer H1, Lamborghini Murcielago, and Bentley Continental.

STRIDER
DIDN'T MISS A BEAT

2 This is only rewarded to you if you beat the Balrog without falling, and you won't be able to replay the Balrog section without making your way through the entire game again! Because of that, if you do fall, quit out and then continue, as this will put you back at the start of the Balrog section. Otherwise, use your double jump and teleport to kill the enemies and land on each platform.

VOLGARR THE VIKING
RED MEANS DEAD

3 This is a notoriously hard achievement, and earning Ending A, needed to unlock Red Means Dead, isn't easy. Players need to complete all six worlds, complete Yggdrasil's roots, collect enough Warrior Spirits, and work through the upper path to continue on Path of the Valkyrie.

GRIM FANDANGO
THE RIGHT WAY

4 This is more of an annoying trophy than a particularly difficult one. To unlock it, you have to play the entire game using the original tank controls, where you rotate on the spot before walking in a direction. It's a little awkward and it can be frustrating at times, but it's well worth persisting with, because you get a gold trophy for your hard work!

VELOCITY 2X
FUTURLAB CERTIFIED

5 This sci-fi shooter is a real challenge, and to get FuturLab Certified, you need to be extremely quick with your reactions. You need to gain 50 perfect medals to unlock this achievement, and the requirements are beating the level under the gold time, rescuing all the survivors, collecting all crystals, beating the high score, *and* not dying. Oh, and this all has to be done on the same run-through on that particular level. Ouch!

FORZA HORIZON 2
WORTHY OF A SULTAN

6 This achievement demands that you have 175 cars in your garage. Sounds like a lot, right? Fortunately, duplicates of cars count toward your total, so you could buy 175 Volkswagen Rabbit GTIs (the cheapest car in *Forza Horizon 2*) and need only $875,000 in total to get this achievement. You can also unlock a perk that gives you a 10 percent discount on cars, and if you get a duplicate car during a free spin, don't sell it, hang on to it.

MINECRAFT
ON A RAIL

7 Nothing in *Minecraft* is incredibly difficult, but this is a time-consuming achievement. You need to travel by mine cart to a point 500 m in a single direction from where you start. To do this, you need 18 powered rails, 496 normal rails, and a mine cart. So, in total, you need 3 redstone, 34 sticks, 18 gold bars, and 186 iron bars. Build a power rail for every 31 normal rails . . . or, if you're really lucky, join someone who already has a rail track built, so you can ride theirs to earn the accolade!

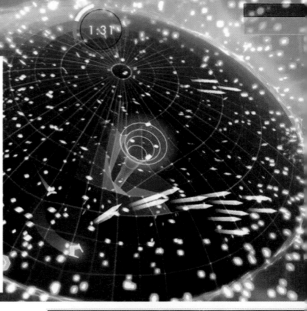

OLD-SKOOL ACHIEVEMENT!

PORTAL
APERTURE SCIENCE

8 If you think you've mastered Valve's classic puzzle game, then tackle the Aperture Science Achievement, awarded to those who have earned a gold medal on all *Portal* challenges. It's incredibly tough and there's no shortcut to success here, but stick with it—the more practice you put in, the better your *Portal* technique becomes and the easier this achievement will seem!

GEOMETRY WARS 3: DIMENSIONS
SURVIVALIST

10 All the challenges that are unlocked in Pacificism Classic mode are tough, and Survivalist could be the toughest one of all. The trick is to learn how the blue diamonds move and then "circle" them, leading them into a bigger cluster while avoiding the gates. Remember that while you can hit gates after 30 seconds expire, you still need to finish the game for the achievement or trophy to unlock.

STEAMWORLD DIG
MASTER PROSPECTOR

11 To get the four gold stars needed for this tough trophy, you need to complete the game without dying while collecting 150 blue orbs and $20,000. Oh, and you need to do this in less than two and a half hours. The trick is to get to Old World and Vectron first, work backward to Archea, and not bother upgrading the Pickaxe.

NBA 2K14
COLLECT 'EM ALL

9 There's nothing worse than an achievement or trophy that relies heavily on luck, and that's precisely what makes this one such a nuisance. The task is simple enough—all you have to do is collect all the player cards to complete all team rosters for the '13–'14 season. But here's the catch: Like *FIFA*'s Ultimate Team players, NBA stars are awarded at random when booster packs are opened. All you can really do is grind out the necessary currency or bite the bullet and spend some real cash. Unless you do, you'll never get this . . .

OCTODAD: DADLIEST CATCH
DANCING IN THE DARK

12 This dancing minigame comes at a point in the game at which you should be comfortable controlling the crazy octopus at the heart of *Octodad*, but even so, this can be an awkward challenge! Be quick, and remember that you don't have to stand on each square as it lights up—you just need to touch it.

SUPER T.I.M.E. FORCE
THEY ARE LOOKING

13 This secret achievement is tough. First you need to find the "Looker," a collection of squares by the level. When you grab it, you need to rewind right back to the start of the level. You'll now have 20 seconds to grab the collectible shards on the level AND reach the Looker for a second time. Doing so will unlock this achievement. Very difficult!

THE ESCAPISTS
THE ESCAPIST!

14 This game asks you to escape from all six prisons to unlock the Escapist! There are different ways of doing this, but the easiest is to knock all the guards out so the door opens. Give the other inmates gifts so they like you, and create a Whip (Timber + Wire + Razor Blade) and Plated Inmate Outfit (Inmate Outfit + Duct Tape + Sheet of Metal) before causing mayhem.

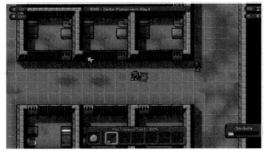

FINAL FANTASY X HD
LIGHTNING DANCER

15 When *Final Fantasy X* was first released, dodging the lightning on the Thunder Plains was notoriously one of the trickiest things to do. Now there's an entire trophy dedicated to dodging 200 of them! Wearing armor with No Encounters ability makes this easier, but don't leave the area or save during your attempt, since this will reset the lightning dodge count.

SKYLANDERS: TRAP TEAM
DREAM A LITTLE NIGHTMARE

16 Unless you've got a small army of plastic friends on hand, beating Trap Team on Nightmare difficulty is no easy feat. The last fight in particular is absolutely brutal—the easiest way is to get a Kaos trap, capture him on Normal, then use him against himself!

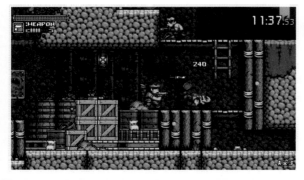

MERCENARY KINGS
DECORATOR

17 The bulk of the trophies in *Mercenary Kings* will see you grinding for items to craft mods, parts, knives, and so on. A quick tip to save you time is creating a backup of your save file on a USB stick and then, after crafting for items and unlocking the relevant trophies, reverting back to your save file so you have all your items again. Easy!

DID YOU KNOW?

Unlocking "entitlements" doesn't sound so cool, does it? Sony's in-game rewards were once rumored to be called entitlements, until Sony confirmed the rewards would be called trophies.

50 HARDEST ACHIEVEMENTS & TROPHIES

OLD-SKOOL ACHIEVEMENT!

VIVA PIÑATA
EVOLVER

19 This one isn't particularly taxing once you know what to do, but how to evolve the cute, candy-filled residents of your garden is never actually explained. Methods are often obtuse to the point that you'd never figure them out without a guide (like feeding a Lickatoad a poisonous fruit, then hitting it with a spade, or setting a Taffly on fire, then putting it out using the watering can) but if you can at least do those two, you'll get your achievement.

GUACAMELEE!: SUPER TURBO CHAMPIONSHIP EDITION
WORLD CHAMPION

18 Can you get a gold medal for all the Infierno challenges in El Diablo's domain? It's really tough, but remember to use the roll to bypass any obstacles, and hold on to your Intenso meter for when you really need it (if you're about to drop a combo, about to die, etc.). It doesn't recharge between failed attempts, so build it up before taking on these really hard challenges!

PINBALL FX 2
POWER OF A GOD

20 This trophy for the Infinity Gauntlet table has been unlocked by only 0.1 percent of those who have tried it. To get the trophy, you need to claim all the Infinity Gems, then defeat Thanos. Practice on easier tables to sharpen your skills, then memorize the table notes in the menus so you know how and where to trigger all the special modes.

CASTLESTORM: DEFINITIVE EDITION
ALL-STAR

21 This tower defense game awards you the All-Star accomplishment when you hit 100 percent completion in Campaign Mode. The easiest way to do this is by focusing on upgrading your Tri-Stone shot first, as this will allow you to blitz through the majority of levels with ease (except ones where Tri-Stone is disabled—simply revisit these later when you've upgraded your other weapons and soldiers).

DON'T STARVE
THE SILENT

22 You need to unlock Wes to get this trophy. To do so, you need to break the Maxwell Statues in the third chapter of Adventure Mode, beat the Clockwork Monsters, then clear the Bishops, Knights, and Rooks in the chamber where Wes is trapped. Pretty tough, right? That's why this trophy has been unlocked by only 0.1 percent of *Don't Starve*'s players to date . . .

INJUSTICE: GODS AMONG US
ULTIMATE BATTLER

23 The trickiest challenge in STAR Labs that stands between you and the Ultimate Battler Trophy is "Impossible." However, you can make life much easier for yourself by picking Hawkgirl, jumping backward, and pressing Back, Forward, 2. This special move does plenty of damage even if they block, and it keeps you relatively safe. You'll need luck, because unlocking this achievement or trophy ultimately depends on the AI being stumped by your tactics—but hey, what tough challenge doesn't require divine intervention?

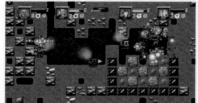

SUPER MOTHERLOAD
CHEAT DEATH

24 You need to complete *Super Motherload* on Hardcore mode to unlock this trophy, which sounds fine in theory . . . except that in Hardcore mode, you die as soon as you run out of fuel. Ouch. Practice a lot, and hope for some luck.

TOWERFALL ASCENSION
MASTER MYTHOLOGY

25 This trophy is unlocked after you clock up a staggering 20,000 rounds of Versus mode. 20,000 rounds! It's not that this trophy is difficult to unlock—it's more that few will have the insane dedication required to play the required number of rounds . . .

OLD-SKOOL ACHIEVEMENT!

50 HIT STREAK

DJ HERO
TURNTABLE PERFECTION

26 Unless you've got an ear for music and hands that can move like lightning, just forget about this one right now. The task here is to earn five stars on every mix in the game on Expert difficulty, where the speedy note highway and complex pattern demand both skill and practice. Even if you do manage to get really good, the last couple of sets of songs are so rough that just one slipup can throw you off enough to make it near impossible to hit five stars. The trick here is to ace rewinds on easy passages with lots of notes for maximum points. Good luck!

PLANTS VS. ZOMBIES GARDEN WARFARE
GARDEN CRAZY

27 Garden Ops is a tough nut to crack, which is why Garden Crazy is awarded only to those who complete this mode on Crazy difficulty. Play as the Pea Shooter and use your Hyper ability to either run away from trouble or jump up onto difficult-to-reach areas, and remember that more players might not help, since the number of zombies increases for each player who has joined the fight alongside you!

DESTINY
FLAWLESS RAIDER

28 One of the main reasons this is so difficult is that it doesn't matter how good you get—any one of your allies could mess up during a Raid, and you'll all miss out on the trophy or achievement. To beat a Raid without dying, we suggest running Vault of Glass often and with a regular group until everyone knows *exactly* what they're doing. Then set aside an evening for your flawless run attempt(s). If anyone goes down, keep your cool, return to Orbit, and try again.

DID YOU KNOW?
The first-ever PlayStation game with unlockable trophies was the downloadable PSN game *Super Stardust HD*, which was released back in June 2008, almost two years after the PlayStation 3 launched!

OLD-SKOOL ACHIEVEMENT!

ROCK BAND 2
THE BLADDER OF STEEL AWARD

29 Endless Setlist 2 in *Rock Band 2* gives you 84 songs, back to back, which totals almost seven hours of music. To get this award, you have to complete Endless Setlist 2 without a single break. No failing. No pausing to go to the bathroom. Just straight-up rocking out for almost seven hours. We'd suggest trying this on the bass route—it's easier—and make sure you use fresh batteries before attempting it! The batteries running out counts as a pause.

KNACK
KNACK MASTER

30 It may not look like it, but this PS4 exclusive can be tricky at times. For this trophy, you'll need to finish the game on the unlockable Very Hard difficulty. You'll need to gain access to Diamond Knack to stand a chance, and even then, enemies still pack a punch. We suggest doing your Very Hard run as soon as you can after unlocking Diamond Knack, just so the levels are all still fresh in your mind.

THE BINDING COIL COMPLETE!

FINAL FANTASY XIV
SEEKER OF TRUTH

31 You need to clear the Binding Coil to get this trophy, and it's one of the toughest challenges to overcome in the entire game. Make sure your item level is 80 or higher (you want nearly full Mythology Armor), and communicate with your group. Understanding your role and that of others is vital.

TRIALS FUSION
THROUGH THE FIRES OF HELL

32 Inferno IV is the hardest track in *Trials Fusion*. It's unlocked by earning 110 medals and completing the Greater Crater, and you need to complete Inferno IV in less than 30 minutes with less than 500 faults to earn Through the Fires of Hell as your reward. Practice, practice, practice is the only way to get through this track while hitting the necessary requirements, and selecting Pit Viper as your bike will make life a tiny fraction easier.

DRIVECLUB
CLEANUP

33 This can be tricky, as you need to finish on the podium without losing any "Fame" due to collisions with other racers. To make life easier for yourself, we suggest that you create a Solo Event on your favorite track (make sure you know it well!), and keep the race slow—set the difficulty to Rookie and choose a Hot Hatch Car. You can go offtrack and collide with obstacles, but remember to avoid other cars. You only need to finish on the podium, so don't take silly risks, since you don't have to finish first in order to grab this trophy.

OLD-SKOOL ACHIEVEMENT!

1000 Note Streak!

GUITAR HERO III: LEGENDS OF ROCK
THE INHUMAN ACHIEVEMENT

34 Think you're good at *Guitar Hero*? Prove it to the world by grabbing this achievement, earned by clearing the ridiculously tough bonus song, *Through the Fire and Flames* by Dragonforce. Put it this way—most people can't even get through the intro. To do so, you're going to need to abuse hammer-ons and pull-offs and use both hands on the fret buttons after strumming the first note. If you can get into the song (and strum fast), only the solos should really present a problem. But there are quite a few . . .

SPELUNKY
TO HELL AND BACK

35 To complete the game the hard way, you need to do the following. Grab the Udjat Eye from the mines and use it to find the entrance to the Black Market in the jungle. Buy or steal the Ankh from the Black Market, take it to the big blue stone head in the Ice Caves, and die next to it. From inside the stone head, you need to grab the Hedjet helmet. Kill Anubis in the Temple, grab his Scepter, and take it to the golden door in the City of Gold. Here, take the Book of Dead, and when it starts laughing, you'll be above the entrance to Hell. You need Olmec to fall into the level below this area, and use the top of his head to enter Hell. Hell is home to King Yama, the boss you need to beat to get To Hell and Back. A lot of work for a simple reward!

RESIDENT EVIL
CQC FTW

36 The original survival horror game has returned in HD, and it has a tough list of challenges, the toughest being CQC FTW—completing the game using only the knife. That means no other weapons, no lighter, no defensive items, no stomping zombie heads! This was known as one of the toughest accolades in gaming before the achievements system even existed; fans took pride in mastering *Resident Evil* to the point where they could complete knife-only runs. So this is one of the most prestigious achievements around.

50 HARDEST ACHIEVEMENTS & TROPHIES

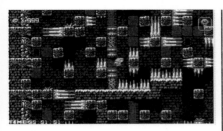

1001 SPIKES
SPEED RUNNER

37 This will push your platforming skills to their limit, thanks to the deadly traps throughout the game that will kill you at a moment's notice. That is why the Speed Runner Trophy is so difficult—completing every stage of the game as Aban Hawkins is hard enough, but doing it with a cumulative time of less than 30 minutes? Good luck!

ROGUE LEGACY
THANATOPHOBIA

38 Without using the Architect, you need to complete *Rogue Legacy* dying just 15 times or fewer for this trophy. Tips? Leaving rooms resets enemy positions; don't smash statues unless you need to; collect gold to spend on health and damage upgrades; and take your time. There's no shortcut to this trophy, so keep trying.

JUST DANCE 2014
EPIC DANCE CREW

39 As with *Destiny*'s Flawless Raider, you're relying on other people here—you'll need to do a four-player song and each get five stars, which means there's not a lot of room for error . . . or a lot of room in general, with four people strutting their stuff! Just pick an easy song or one you all know well, then keep doing it until you all ace it.

STRIKE SUIT ZERO
STRIKE FAST

40 Can you complete the last mission in seven minutes? You can if you skip the cut scenes, use thrusters, and destroy the core rather than the limiter path. Also, when you get close to the core, make sure you use the Strike Mode gun rather than the missiles, which can be inconsistent. Do all that and you should complete the last mission in under seven minutes, earning you Strike Fast!

STICK IT TO THE MAN
THE BIRD IN THE SKY

41 You have to sneak past the helicopter in chapter 7 without being spotted to unlock this, and there's a little trick to make it easier. Ordinarily, if you're spotted, you have to replay the chapter again from the start. Instead, immediately force quit the game, load it back up, and reload your save. This will put you at the last checkpoint, allowing you to try again without much progress lost!

GOAT SIMULATOR
THE FLAPMASTER

42 There are lots of quirky achievements in *Goat Simulator* that aren't too difficult but do require specific knowledge. For example, to unlock the bizarrely named Rymdskepp i Rymden achievement, players need to find the beacon in the garage behind the spawn point and drag it to the crop circle. For the Angel Goat achievement, they just need to behave themselves for five minutes. But the Flapmaster? That does take skill! This *Flappy Bird* spoof can be found upstairs in the Coffee House. Players have to clear out the room first, since they want a clear view before they start playing, then start. Their hit box is bigger than it seems, but the only way to nail this achievement is to keep practicing!

DID YOU KNOW?

Microsoft's "achievements" system launched alongside Xbox 360, and it was in *King Kong: The Official Game of the Movie* that most gamers earned their first full 1,000 gamerscore.

OLLIOLLI 2: WELCOME TO OLLIWOOD
I WANT IT ALL

43 Skating games have never been particularly easy, and this one is no exception. To unlock this, you need to do *everything*—smash high scores, ace all the RAD mode levels (which are stupidly tough), and complete every challenge. Whoa . . .

PEGGLE 2
ALL THE CHEEVOS!

44 You've truly mastered *Peggle 2* if you complete all the optional challenges to grab this elusive trophy. We suggest using Gnorman, as he's the most versatile, and always leave a single orange peg as high as you can for your last shot when going for a "Clear All Pegs" objective.

EA SPORTS UFC
IT'S SHOWTIME!

45 This is unlocked for knocking your opponent out with a cage kick, which has to be the flashiest way of ending the match! To give yourself the best chance of pulling off this feat, choose Anthony Pettis and attack the head until it turns red in the damage indicator. Then go for the cage kick, which is done by pressing the right bumper, pushing away from your opponent, and pressing Kick. Some luck is involved, but if you've done enough damage, the cage kick should land you the KO.

FINAL FANTASY TYPE-0 HD
PERFECT MARKS

46 You'll struggle to get an S rank in any mission in the main game without grinding and leveling *way* more than you should. Luckily, there's an easy way to land this otherwise tricky trophy. All you need to do is wait until later in the game when your whole team is suitably powered up, then drop the difficulty level down to Easy and replay an early mission.

It was here that Class Zero made its first mark in the pages of history.

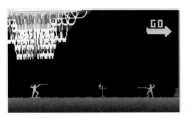

NIDHOGG
HOGGLIKE

47 All the trophies for *Nidhogg* are fairly easy except for this one, which demands that you complete single player without dying *or* losing the arrow. You have to get this trophy in a single run, which makes it even harder, but practicing the campaign over and over and over again will help you finish it in around 15 minutes, making this trophy less of a time drain than it would be if you messed up at any point.

THE BEST GAMERS IN THE WORLD?

STALLION83

Who are the best Xbox One and PS4 gamers in the world, if you go by their gamerscores or trophy counts? On Xbox One, it's Stallion83, who was the first gamer in the world to crack the mythical 1 million gamerscore barrier. Not satisfied with reaching that milestone, Stallion83 has since become the first gamer to breach 1,100,000 gamerpoints, too. Meanwhile, on PSN, Hakoom became the first gamer to hit trophy level 100, which took five years of trophy hunting and some 30,000 trophies to accomplish. His feat was so unusual that Sony then lifted the level 100 trophy cap. Hakoom has continued demolishing PlayStation games since then, unlocking an average of 16 trophies a day.

HOW DO YOU COMPARE TO THESE TWO LEGENDS OF GAMING?

PES 2015
NO. 1 CLUB

48 The ultimate accomplishment in *PES 2015* is becoming the number one ranked club in Master League mode. It's important to note that this isn't awarded based on your number of wins or titles, but rather on how good your squad is. Target free agents with high overall ratings after each season and cut loose any players who fall short. It'll take a few seasons to get this, so keep at it.

RAYMAN LEGENDS
TRULY AWESOME!

49 You haven't finished *Rayman Legends* until you reach the final level of Awesomeness, which triggers this achievement. If you get all diamond cups, you're left with 1,816 points to go, which means you have to turn to the daily and weekly challenges. It's a grind to get this done—it'll take roughly 12 weeks of doing challenges if you consistently get gold rankings—but no one said it would be easy, right?

FROM THE HARDEST TO THE EASIEST ...

PRESS START TO PLAY: EASIEST. ACHIEVEMENT. EVER.

PHEW! You'll want a break after scorching your fingers on the red-hot challenges these achievements and trophies have posed. The good news is that *The Simpsons Game* provides just such a break. The game based on Springfield's famous family is generous enough to give out its first achievement the moment you press the Start button. There are some trickier ones later on, sure, but you deserve this for all your hard work with these challenges. **Woo-hoo!**

WWE 2K15
BEST IN THE WORLD!

50 With all the bugs and glitches, we guess you'd be lucky to get through all 19 matches in the "Hustle, Loyalty, Disrespect" 2K Showcase event at all, let alone on Legend difficulty. Still, even this cloud has a silver lining, in the form of a bug that works in your favor! You only have to do the last match on Legend difficulty—smash through the rest on Easy and switch for the last match.

TOP 10 BESTSELLING GAMES EVER

DID YOU KNOW?

Wii Sports came bundled with every Wii in the West, accounting for many of its sales. It wasn't bundled in Japan, though, where nearly 4 million gamers bought it separately.

WII SPORTS

WHY: 82.5 MILLION COPIES SOLD

It's easy to look back at *Wii Sports* and say it's too simple. But the reason it's the bestselling console game ever is because it brought gaming to new people. There aren't many games influential enough to sell a whole console on their own . . .

SUPER MARIO BROS.

WHY: 40.2 MILLION COPIES SOLD

Super Mario Bros. was the first side-scrolling platformer to star Nintendo's mascot. Released on the Nintendo Entertainment System back in 1985, it may be the most influential game ever.

MINECRAFT

WHY: 54 MILLION COPIES SOLD

Chances are, you've had at least one quick look at Mojang's world-building phenomenon. *Minecraft* started off as a humble demo in 2009, but strong word of mouth quickly increased its popularity. Now you'll struggle to find anyone who *hasn't* heard of *Minecraft!*

MARIO KART WII

WHY: 35.5 MILLION COPIES SOLD

Gamers have been enjoying *Mario Kart* since 1992, but the Wii offering is the most popular to date. That's partly because of the Wii Wheel, a handy chunk of plastic you could clip a Wii Remote to. It didn't hurt that its online races were seriously fun.

GRAND THEFT AUTO V

WHY: 45 MILLION COPIES SOLD

Rockstar's ultraviolent crime opus is the fastest-selling game of all time, with over 11 million copies sold in just 24 hours. While some play it for the story line, most gamers just use it to explore.

TETRIS

WHY: 35 MILLION COPIES SOLD

The Game Boy version of the world-famous Russian puzzler was the one that made *Tetris* a household name. Just as *Wii Sports* sold countless Wiis on its own, people of all ages bought Game Boys just so they could play *Tetris* on them—and with good reason.

WII SPORTS RESORT

WHY: 32.5 MILLION COPIES SOLD

Proving that the first *Wii Sports* game wasn't a fluke, the sequel sold more copies than many *consoles* do in their lifetimes. The main reason for this was simple: It came with the new Wii MotionPlus, which allowed for more realistic motion tracking—perfect for the sword-fighting minigame that became its highlight event.

NEW SUPER MARIO BROS.

WHY: 30.75 MILLION COPIES SOLD

The Nintendo DS is the bestselling games system of all time, so it's no surprise that its only side-scrolling *Mario* platformer was an incredibly popular game. Add to that the fact that it was the first new 2-D *Super Mario Bros.* in a stunning 14 years, and you had a game that longtime Nintendo fans and newcomers alike flocked to.

WII PLAY

WHY: 28.8 MILLION COPIES SOLD

The Wii was swamped with minigame collections over the course of its life, so why did *Wii Play* do so much better than the rest? One main reason: It came bundled with a Wii Remote. When the Wii launched, both the console and extra remotes sold out everywhere, so for many gamers, buying *Wii Play* was the only way to get their hands on extra controllers for multiplayer gameplay.

NEW SUPER MARIO BROS. WII

WHY: 27.9 MILLION COPIES SOLD

As with its DS brother, when this was released on the Wii, gamers came out in droves to buy it. This was the first *Mario* platformer to feature co-op play for up to four people, meaning that the entire family could work together as Mario, Luigi, Toad, and, well, another Toad . . .

THE EXPERT SAYS . . .
MIKE BITHELL
Creator of Thomas Was Alone

TETRIS

SUPER MARIO WORLD

My little sister had a Game Boy. It was yellow and fantastic, and it was hers. For the longest time, she had only two games, *Super Mario World* and *Tetris*. I remember playing *Tetris* for hours. I was awful, but that loop was brilliant: a slow-motion fall from grace, starting off strong and confident before sliding, inevitably, into a mess of gaps and mistakes. It was awesome, and it was my obsession for a long time. I ended up claiming that Game Boy as my own, and proceeded to buy more games, but *Tetris* was rarely disconnected for long.

TOP 6 VIDEO-GAME COSPLAYS

RATCHET FROM *RATCHET & CLANK* BY IRON MANDA
WHY: WHAT A LOMBAX LOOKS LIKE IN REAL LIFE!
An incredible fusion of fabric, body paint, fur, and a truly excellent prop. There's something to be said for getting in character and capturing Ratchet's trademark smirk!

© Smallfry Creations

© AgentSakur9

TALIM FROM *SOUL CALIBUR* BY CHERRY TEA COSPLAY
WHY: THE PRIESTESS OF THE WINDS TRANSCENDS TIME AND SPACE
This is the second time that Cherry Tea has created a Talim outfit, and a few extra years of costuming experience has allowed her to pull off a stunning version of the character. Armed with her (con-safe) bladed tonfa and a good photographer, she is ready to eternally retell the tale of souls and swords.

© Paul Beard Photography

ZINOGRE ARMOR FROM *MONSTER HUNTER* BY AURORE COSPLAY
WHY: THE ARMOR IS NOT JUST FOR SHOW
There are some frankly ridiculous armor sets in the *MonHun* series. Aurore's first set of armor, made of special moldable craft plastic, took her the better part of a year to complete. Subtle makeup and the wig help bring out the character.

PRINCESS ZELDA FROM *THE LEGEND OF ZELDA* BY DARKERLINK COSPLAY

WHY: THAT'S A SMASHING COLOR ON YOU

Affectionately known as Red Zelda to DarkerLink, this Zelda wears an outfit based on one of her alternative colors in *Super Smash Bros.*, complete with her Light Bow Final Smash for a guaranteed KO. Alts are great for different versions of a character or an excuse to keep dressing as your favorite character.

© ManyLemons – ManyLemons.co.uk

© RBF-Productions-NL

AVELINE DE GRANDPRÉ FROM *ASSASSIN'S CREED* BY DOMINIQUE BOER

WHY: YOU'LL NEVER SEE HER COMING

For some cosplayers, sewing a costume is only one piece of the puzzle. This full Aveline costume by RBF-Productions-NL is not only beautifully made but also incorporates insane attention to detail, like the weathering and fading that make it look like the well-worn clothes of a busy Louisianan assassin.

© Zero Destiny Photography

GABRANTH FROM *FINAL FANTASY XII* BY THE MYSTERIOUS COSPLAYER

WHY: WHO IS BEHIND THAT EXCELLENT MASK?

The iconic helmet in the *Final Fantasy XII* logo comes from a character in the game, represented here by the Mysterious Cosplayer. It's an incredibly convincing costume, but it's not actually metal. Good thing, too—a plate-metal suit of armor of that size would not be easy to walk in.

THE EXPERT SAYS . . .

LAURA SINDALL

Euro Cosplay Gathering Champion 2014 (www.LauraSindall.com)

© Colin J Smith

Cosplay is a wonderful, creative hobby that you can enjoy with other like-minded people at conventions all across the world. For me, the challenge of learning about new skills and materials to bring a character to life has always brought me great joy, even more so when I get to travel and compete in contests abroad, allowing me to meet so many cosplayers from other countries who share this great passion. I don't think you would find many other hobbies that create such close friendships with such enthusiastically creative people from all over the world.

TOP 10 COOLEST WEAPONS

RED SHELL (MARIO KART)

WHY: Show us a person who hasn't been zinged out of first place by a well-timed red shell and we'll show you a liar! No matter which game in the *Mario Kart* series you're playing, the red shell is to be feared.

MR. ZURKON (RATCHET & CLANK)

WHY: He's "the perfect companion for spontaneous treks through hostile environments"! Though Mr. Zurkon is teeny and tiny and all kinds of cute, his laser mercilessly cuts down anything unfortunate enough to be in his path. And if the laser isn't sharp enough, Mr. Zurkon's insulting put-downs just might finish the job! Yup, Mr. Zurkon's "currency is pain"—that's why he's one of our favorite allies in a fight! He even made a return in other *Ratchet & Clank* titles.

MORPH-O-RAY (RATCHET & CLANK)

WHY: It might not look like the most impressive weapon, but once you start tinkering with it, the Morph-O-Ray is brilliant. Adding mods helps you tailor your gun to certain situations. And then there's the Dark Mod . . . Oh, how we love the Dark Mod!

KEYBLADE (KINGDOM HEARTS)

WHY: As swords go, this is undoubtedly one of gaming's coolest offerings. Sure, it's shaped like a key, and that's cool, but don't think that's all the Keyblade has to offer! Buff your abilities, "unlock" new worlds, and enhance the damage you dole out to enemies.

PORTAL GUN (PORTAL)

WHY: Hard to believe that a gun that doesn't require reloading or extra ammo clips can make such an impact, but the Portal gun is a huge part of what makes *Portal* so absorbing. It allows you to travel vast distances in an instant—we're happiest when thinking with Portals!

POKÉ BALL (POKÉMON)

WHY: Some may argue that this isn't a weapon, but we're inclined to disagree. It looks harmless, but the Poké Ball can capture your opponents, making it the most important tool you have available. Think of it like this: Is there anything in gaming that carries as much importance as the Poké Ball does to *Pokémon* players?

RYNO V (RATCHET & CLANK)

WHY: Another entry from the *Ratchet & Clank* series? The RYNO V is one of gaming's most powerful weapons, and certainly one of the most iconic items in the series. Essentially a gigantic rocket launcher, it fires heat-seeking ammo at will, wiping out anything in its path. Even better is the sweet music that plays when you're firing it!

SUPER SHEEP (WORMS)

WHY: This is the part where we're supposed to tell you all the reasons why the super sheep is awesome, but . . . come on! It's a SHEEP. A SUPER sheep! A super sheep that you can fire at your enemies! Okay, so sometimes when it flies majestically through the air, it falls and kills your own squad . . . but who cares?! Death by flying super sheep surely has to be a truly magnificent way to go, right?!

CONCRETE DONKEY (WORMS)

WHY: While we're on the subject of weapons from the *Worms* series, the only thing better than a super sheep is a gigantic concrete donkey. Getting one isn't always easy—it's often a matter of luck when you grab a weapon crate—but the concrete donkey is the deadliest, and most hilarious, weapon in the *Worms* universe! *HEE-HAW!*

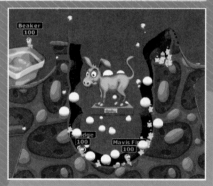

MASTER SWORD (ZELDA)

WHY: A staple of *Zelda* for years, the Master Sword is one of our favorite weapons. While it's true that *Zelda* offers a whole heap of weapons from which to choose, it's the majestic Master Sword that Link must prove his worth to attain. Sometimes permitting time travel or banishing evil, sometimes turning enemies to stone, the Master Sword is one of the most versatile weapons ever!

THE EXPERT SAYS . . .
"WHYBEARE"
YouTuber

SUPER SMASH BROS.

The coolest weapon in gaming is the tree that the Villager uses in *Super Smash Bros.* You would never expect someone to use a whole tree as a weapon against you. Not only can it be used as a weapon when it grows, but it can also be used as a weapon when you cut it down. The only thing cooler than that is Captain Falcon's knee, but that's considered a weapon only in some locations.

THE BEST GAMING UNLOCKABLES

THE BEST GAMING UNLOCKABLES

FLIGHT

FEZ You can actually skip the delicately crafted levels in one of the best puzzle games ever made by flying around when playing through the second time. All you have to do is enter Up, Up, Up + A, and off you go! It won't ruin the game, since you have to have completed *Fez* for this to become available, and it is really good fun!

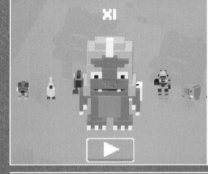

POOPY PIGEON

CROSSY ROAD From Chinese Xi to Poopy Pigeon, from Festive Chicken to Hipster Whale, from Android Robot to Pew Die Pug, few games do unlockable characters as well as the uniquely insane *Crossy Road*. Think of the craziest character you can, and it's likely already in here!

3-D TRAILER

BRAVELY DEFAULT One of the more unusual unlockables comes in the fantastic *Bravely Default* for 3DS, which delighted J-RPG fans last year. Enter the Konami code on the title screen—Up, Up, Down, Down, Left, Right, Left, Right, B, A, Start—and you'll unlock a special 3-D game trailer!

DOUGHNUT DRAKE

UNCHARTED 3: DRAKE'S DECEPTION The rotund version of our favorite hero appears as a multiplayer skin in all three *Uncharted* games and is often the last item you unlock, because Doughnut Drake is usually the most expensive. Who's willing to bet against Doughnut Drake appearing in *Uncharted 4*?

GEOMETRY WARS

PROJECT GOTHAM RACING 3 This shooter was tucked away as an arcade bonus in the garage of *Project Gotham Racing 3*. It was so popular that the effects are still being felt, with the amazing *Geometry Wars 3: Dimensions* now released on Xbox One and PS4 as a stand-alone game!

MR. TOOTS

RED FACTION: ARMAGEDDON The reward for completing *Red Faction: Armageddon* is Mr. Toots, one of the best gaming unlockables of all time. Who is Mr. Toots? He's a colorful unicorn who fires rainbows out his rear as enemies explode into clouds of stars and butterflies.

THE BEST GAMING UNLOCKABLES

RIDICULOUS COSTUMES

PLANTS VS. ZOMBIES GARDEN WARFARE One of the best things about *Plants vs. Zombies Garden Warfare* is the sheer amount of, well, *stuff* you can unlock. There are so many costume variations to play around with—hockey masks, popcorn boxes, frozen faces, cowboy hats with arrows in them, stone skin, 3-D glasses, fiery hands, mad scientist hair, tribal makeup . . . The list goes on and on!

PIE IN FACE

TEKKEN TAG TOURNAMENT 2 *Tekken Tag Tournament 2*, the predecessor to the fabulous *Tekken 7*, provided one of the best unlockables in recent gaming memory. You can buy a pie and wear it on your head . . . and then forcefully splat it into your opponent's face, where it remains for the rest of the match! Is there anything more humiliatingly awesome than smashing baked goods into your foe's face? Doubt it.

Let's see it! Whoa! Dude, that, that's a Lamborghini Miura.

ABANDONED CARS

FORZA HORIZON 2 Dotted around *Forza Horizon 2* are remote barns, which contain abandoned cars. The point of finding these cars? You can scrub them up and bring them back to life, and they're then available to drive for the rest of the game. Best of all, they're unique cars that can't be found any other way. Our own personal favorite is the lightning-fast Lamborghini Miura . . .

COUCH

BATTLEFIELD HARDLINE One of the oddest secrets we've seen in gaming is the drivable couch in *Battlefield Hardline*. Yes, you read that right—drivable couch. It's not just for one player, either—gamers soon discovered they could all pile onto the couch and drive around! It's located only in one map and in one mode, but it deserves a spot on this list just for how utterly surreal it is. It's made even more surreal by how superfast it is.

RESOGUN: HEROES

With two new modes packed into this DLC, Survival and Demolition, *Heroes* is a test of your *Resogun* skills and twitch reactions. With new leaderboards and new enemies to boot, PS4's fastest shooting game is made even better!

DRIVECLUB: WEATHER UPDATE

Technically, we're cheating here. *DriveClub*'s weather update isn't DLC, but the free update is so impressive, we simply have to include it. Is there any game that looks better than *DriveClub* during stormy weather? We think not.

ASSASSIN'S CREED: FREEDOM CRY

This DLC follows Adéwalé, one of the slaves who found freedom as a pirate on the *Jackdaw* before becoming a trained assassin. *Freedom Cry* sees Adéwalé shipwrecked, with no weapon and no crew. Can he survive what lies ahead?

CHILD OF LIGHT: GOLEM'S PLIGHT

The extra character in *Child of Light* provides a whole new challenge, as you have to get used to how slow Golem is as a trade-off for his overpowering attacks. *Golem's Plight* is a fresh way to tackle a fantastic game.

CAPTAIN TOAD

CAPTAIN TOAD:

TREASURE TRACKER
WII U'S CUTE PLATFORMER

It doesn't matter how cold or cynical you might be—the cutesy charm of *Captain Toad* will warm up even the iciest of hearts! Full of secrets and oozing charm, this is an essential Wii U purchase.

FORZA MOTORSPORT

FEEL THE FORZA

FEEL THE FORZA

PlayStation has *Gran Turismo*, so Xbox has *Forza*. That's the way it has been ever since 2005, when the first *Forza Motorsport* roared onto Xbox.

It's a gaming tradition that has continued with Xbox One. *Forza Motorsport 5* stunned racing fans with its gorgeous graphics, and *Forza Horizon 2* allowed them to take part in fun and ridiculous challenges—such as racing against planes! Better yet, there is the Fast & Furious DLC for *Forza Horizon 2*, with cars such as a 2015 Dodge Challenger and a 1970 Plymouth Cuda.

And *Forza Motorsport 6* is on the way, a game that should push the graphics to a whole new level . . .

DID YOU KNOW?
The upcoming *Forza Motorsport 6* has the new Ford GT supercar on the front cover. You'll be able to drive it in the game before the real one's even out!

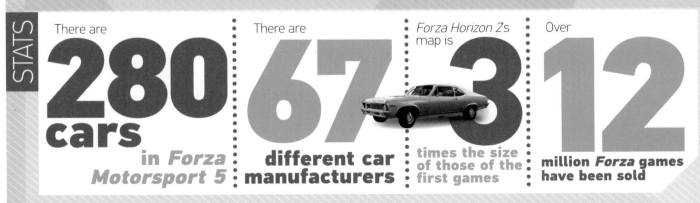

STATS

There are **280 cars** in *Forza Motorsport 5*

There are **67** **different car manufacturers**

Forza Horizon 2's map is **3** **times the size of those of the first games**

Over **12** **million *Forza* games have been sold**

TOP **5** ODDEST FORZA HORIZON 2 CARS

FORD F-100 (1956)

1 *Forza Horizon 2* is packed with awesome supercars, but it also features some stranger vehicles that probably wouldn't be your first choices in a speed race, like this odd Ford pickup truck that is nearly 60 years old!

JEEP WILLYS MB (1945)

2 One of the oldest cars in *Forza Horizon 2*, this old army Jeep can be found in one of the hidden barns dotted around the game's map. Once it's restored, you can potter around in it: As you'd expect, it isn't exactly fast.

HUMMER H1 ALPHA (2006)

3 The Hummer is the biggest car in *Forza Horizon 2*, and it has a real weight to it, too. You'll be safe in the knowledge that the road belongs to you—anyone who tries to nudge you off the road during races is quickly going to regret it!

VOLKSWAGEN TYPE 2 DE LUXE (1963)

4 These little 1960s camper vans can sell for amazingly high prices these days, but definitely not for racing. Perfect for a trip to to the coast, but not so hot when you need to quickly hit 100 miles per hour (160 kph)!

FORD TRANSIT SUPER-SPORTVAN (2011)

5 Think racing games and you think sleek sports cars, with engines that roar and looks that kill. What you don't think of are bulky vans . . . We don't see this vehicle winning too many races any time soon!

95% PROGRESS | POSITION 6/12

TIME LINE

2005	FORZA MOTORSPORT
2007	FORZA MOTORSPORT 2
2009	FORZA MOTORSPORT 3
2011	FORZA MOTORSPORT 4
2012	FORZA HORIZON
2013	FORZA MOTORSPORT 5
2014	FORZA HORIZON 2

ALSO CHECK OUT . . .

DRIVECLUB
Forza's exclusive to Xbox, so if you have a PlayStation 4 and want something similar, *DriveClub* looks and feels just as incredible.

GRAN TURISMO 6
Sony's PS3 racer is the king of content, with an amazing 1,200 cars to choose from and 71 tracks to race them on. Will last hundreds of hours.

THE CREW
If *Forza Horizon*'s open-world racing is more your thing, *The Crew* might be worth a look, with its focus on mission-based races.

GRAN TURISMO

BURNING RUBBER

This series is one of the most important "simulation" racing games, meaning that it takes a more serious approach to driving in games. That might sound a little boring, but it's actually surprisingly exciting: Rather than screeching around corners at ridiculous speeds, players win in *Gran Turismo* by being smart about the way they drive.

Even though it has been out for over a year, *Gran Turismo 6* still receives plenty of new content. Just recently it has received two new Vision GT cars, a special safety car based on the BMW M4, and the fan-favorite Mid-Field Raceway track via free updates.

Perhaps it's just as well there's so much new stuff to get sucked into, since *Gran Turismo 7* isn't due until 2017 . . .

DID YOU KNOW?

Gran Turismo 5's concept car—the Red Bull X2010—was designed in response to this question: If you ignored all rules and regulations, what would the fastest car in the world look like?

STATS

71.35 million copies of the game have been sold

663 kph is the fastest speed possible so far

691 million credits: the total cost of every car in *Gran Turismo 6*

1886: the release year of the **oldest car** included in the series

TOP **5** FASTEST CARS

RED BULL X2010 (GT5)

1 This beast of a machine was added into *Gran Turismo 5* and is easily the fastest car available in the series so far. It was designed exclusively for the game to produce what would be the potential fastest car in the world.

FORMULA GT (GT4)

2 With an astonishing top performance of 936 horsepower, the Formula GT is definitely capable of some incredible speeds. *Gran Turismo* developer Polyphony Digital actually designed this car itself.

TIME LINE

1997 – GRAN TURISMO
1999 – GRAN TURISMO 2
2001 – GRAN TURISMO 3: A-SPEC
2002 – GRAN TURISMO CONCEPT
2003 – GRAN TURISMO 4 PROLOGUE
2005 – GRAN TURISMO 4
2006 – GRAN TURISMO HD
2007 – GRAN TURISMO 5 PROLOGUE
2009 – GRAN TURISMO (PSP)
2010 – GRAN TURISMO 5
2013 – GRAN TURISMO 6

FERRARI ENZO (GT5)

3 The Ferrari Enzo is a little bit awkward to control, meaning that it takes some practice to understand. If you do manage to figure it out, however, it's worth it, as you'll find it's one of the quickest cars available in *Gran Turismo*.

BUGATTI VEYRON (GT5)

4 More of a production model, the Bugatti Veyron might not be able to outclass the likes of the Red Bull X2010 or the Formula GT, but it's still capable of incredibly high speeds—and it's a beautifully designed car, too!

ALSO CHECK OUT . . .

GRAN TURISMO 6
With over 1,200 cars, 100 tracks, and a wide range of different vehicles, this is without a doubt the most varied and complete version of the game.

FORZA MOTORSPORT
The Xbox equivalent for those without PlayStations, this simulation racer is just as good as *Gran Turismo*.

MINOLTA TOYOTA (GT4)

5 This is a sports prototype car, designed *only* for racing on tracks. In fact, sports prototype cars are capable of such speeds that they're not legally allowed to drive on the road! That alone should tell you how fast this one is.

DRIVECLUB
This PS4 exclusive is part simulation, part arcade style, making you race at incredible speeds while still paying attention to cornering.

RACING ROUNDUP

BEST OF THE REST

There's a huge variety of racing games, from arcade racers to simulation, karting to street racing, motorbikes to superpowered race cars. It doesn't matter what you're into, there's a racing game for you. The big names in the genre are the likes of *Need for Speed* and *Burnout*—both of which are more arcade-y in the way they play. Karting games are rarer these days, but they still get some love from *Mario Kart*, *LittleBigPlanet Karting*, and *ModNation Racers*. *DiRT* is a series to keep an eye out for these days, too, offering a much brasher, more exciting approach to contest racing than most games seem to. All you need to do is find the time to try them all!

DID YOU KNOW?

The first racing game was called *Speed Race* and was released by Taito for the arcades in 1974. It came with a steering wheel and was considered innovative for its scrolling graphics.

STATS

There are

5,129

user-created tracks in TrackMania 2 Stadium

The longest track in a racing game is

14.47

miles

Over

13

million copies of *Burnout* have been bought

23

Need for Speed **games have been released**

TOP 5 RACING GAMES TO TRY

BURNOUT PARADISE (2008)

1 Though it's older now, *Burnout Paradise* provides ageless fun. It's an open-world racing game, which was a fairly new concept when it was released. It's an arcade racer with a focus on takedowns.

DIRT 3 (2011)

2 The *DiRT* series started off by targeting rally races but eventually expanded to become a little more about general off-track racing. It's a bit more extreme about drifting than many of its competitors are, but one thing's for certain—it's a brilliant racing game!

RFACTOR 2 (2012)

3 Despite its silly name, *rFactor 2* is considered to be the king of simulation racing games. It's available only on PC, so you'll need a machine capable of running it. But if you're serious about racing games, you should probably try it.

NEED FOR SPEED MOST WANTED (2012)

4 There are a lot of *Need for Speed* games, not all of them that great. *Most Wanted* was the last really impressive one, matching the open world of *Burnout Paradise* with more refined control over the cars.

TRIALS FUSION (2014)

5 Want something different? Try the fiendish *Trials Fusion*, in which the biggest obstacle you face isn't other racers—it's the course. You need to use your balance to stay on your bike while driving as fast as possible. Very tricky stuff!

TIME LINE

Year	Game
1974	SPEED RACE
1974	GRAN TRAK
1976	CRASHING RACE
1976	NIGHT DRIVER
1978	ROAD CHAMPION
1979	MONACO GP
1980	RALLY-X
1982	BUMP N JUMP
1982	POLE POSITION
1983	POLE POSITION 2
1984	EXCITEBIKE
1985	HANG-ON
1986	OUTRUN
1988	CHASE HQ
1989	INDIANAPOLIS 500: THE SIMULATION
1992	VIRTUA RACING
1992	SUPER MARIO KART
1993	RIDGE RACER
1993	DAYTONA USA
1994	THE NEED FOR SPEED
1995	SEGA RALLY CHAMPIONSHIP
1995	WIPEOUT
1997	GRAN TURISMO
1998	COLIN MCRAE RALLY
1999	CRAZY TAXI
1999	MIDTOWN MADNESS
2001	PROJECT GOTHAM RACING
2001	BURNOUT
2005	FORZA MOTORSPORT
2008	RACE DRIVER: GRID
2008	BURNOUT PARADISE
2010	BLUR
2010	MODNATION RACERS
2013	NEED FOR SPEED RIVALS
2014	DRIVECLUB

TOP 8 SHOCKING MOMENTS

STAR WARS: KNIGHTS OF THE OLD REPUBLIC

WHY: The best twist in video-game history

Knights of the Old Republic was an experience, made all the better by one shocking twist: Your character is the bad guy. You're kidnapped by Jedi before the game's start; it's your decision whether to continue as a nice guy or go back to your evil ways!

DID YOU KNOW?

The Legend of Zelda: Majora's Mask's shocking three-day cycle—you have to restart the game once it completes—was originally meant to last a week.

CALL OF DUTY 4: MODERN WARFARE

WHY: Taking risks that others don't

One of the most memorable surprises came in *Modern Warfare*, when *COD* took events to a new level by setting off a nuclear weapon halfway through. Shockingly, the blast killed one of *COD's* main characters.

FINAL FANTASY VII

WHY: The shock death of a main character

Although it's more common now, there was a time when main characters were killed off only when you saw the "Game Over" screen. *Final Fantasy VII* was different—it decided to kill Aeris halfway through. It was *Final Fantasy's* boss Sephiroth who was responsible. All the more reason to defeat him!

BRAID

WHY: The bad guy . . . is none other than you

Braid's final level sees a knight clutching the princess before she breaks free. You try to catch up with her as she unblocks the obstacles in your path. Except . . . it's then revealed that she's running *away* from you and triggering obstacles to slow you down, and the knight is the one saving her!

BIOSHOCK

WHY: It tricked players for the entire game

BioShock's revelation was that the main character was being controlled by someone else. Jack explores the depths of Rapture with the help of Atlas and his repeated phrase of "Would you kindly . . ."—but it turns out that these words are deliberate, used to make Jack obey Atlas's every bidding. With an absorbing backstory revolving around the history of the city and hypnosis, this game is truly shocking.

METROID

WHY: The moment games changed forever

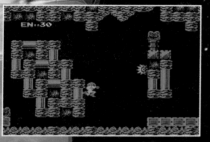

When games were still evolving, women were treated mostly as damsels in distress. That's why it was such a shock when the main character of *Metroid* took his helmet off to reveal that he was in fact a woman. At no time was it expected, or even hinted at, that the soon-to-be-named Samus Aran was female, but it was an important moment in games. The only thing was, you had to finish the game to find out.

HALO: REACH

WHY: No matter what, it's unwinnable

Halo is one of the biggest franchises in gaming. As such, most entries within it end on a somewhat happy note. That's not the case with *Reach*. It tells the story of the last Spartans, and the final level is their last stand against overwhelming odds. There's no way to actually be victorious—meaning that even if players could avoid defeat for hours and hours, eventually they would be overrun by enemy troops.

P.T.

WHY: It's a secret demo for a famous franchise

Nothing is simple with *P.T.* Not only did this demo shock PS4 owners when it was released for free on Sony's online store, it turned out to be an announcement for *Silent Hills*, a new entry in Konami's dormant horror series. But the shocks didn't end there—a few months later, Konami canceled *Silent Hills* with little explanation, and also removed *P.T.* from Sony's online store!

IT'S NOT JUST GAMES THAT HAVE SHOCKED US . . .

Moments in the games industry that left us openmouthed this year!

NINTENDO GOES MOBILE

Mario on mobile? It could happen! Nintendo announced to the world that it would be working with a mobile-games specialist in Japan to bring its much-loved characters to smartphones.

METAL GEAR CREATOR LEAVES

The *Metal Gear* series has always been driven by the crazy genius of creator Hideo Kojima . . . but not for much longer, since he announced that the next *Metal Gear* game will be his last!

ROCK BAND COMES BACK

Plastic guitars were left behind with the Xbox 360 and PS3, right? Apparently not! *Rock Band* master Harmonix is currently working on *Rock Band 4*, so you can become a next-gen guitar god.

LITTLEBIGPLANET

ZIP-A-DEE-DOO-DAH

It's incredible to think that a cloth figurine with no nose could conquer the world, but that's exactly what Sackboy, star of Sony's *LittleBigPlanet* series, has managed to pull off.

The recently released *LittleBigPlanet 3* allowed players to use 16 layers to create their own levels, as opposed to the previous 3. Fans could also create their own power-ups for the first time ever, and they could even create levels that let them switch between different characters. This opened up a whole new world of possibilities in *LittleBigPlanet 3*. It's a game that never feels old, since the servers are stuffed with brand-new levels created by the community!

DID YOU KNOW?

LittleBigPlanet is narrated by Stephen Fry, while the villain in *LittleBigPlanet 3*, Newton, is voiced by Hugh Laurie from *House*.

STATS

Average score of **88** on Metacritic

Over **10** million copies sold worldwide

Over **8** million levels created

The original won **18** awards

TOP **5** CUSTOM LEVELS

LITTLEBIGPLANET

SHADOW OF THE COLOSSUS

1 This cute take on the PS2 epic captures everything that made that game so awesome—finding the colossus, climbing him, taking care of both stamina and wind before striking the weak spot.

TRAFFIC PANIC

2 A simple but perfectly put together minigame, this asks you to direct traffic without causing any crashes to score points. It's like a modern take on retro classic *Frogger*, but with much better graphics.

LOOK BEHIND YOU

3 A first-person horror game? In *LittleBigPlanet*? It's a brilliant mix of cutesy and creepy, blending head-scratching puzzles, smart level design, and use of darkness to keep you on your toes as you make your way through the stage.

CARGO PLANE

4 This is something all PlayStation fans will recognize, as it takes the cargo plane set piece from *Uncharted 3* and re-creates it, complete with the punch-out at the back end of the plane and dodging the crates flying outside!

ACROBATIC RAGDOLL FIGHTER

5 Two warriors battle each other until one stands tall, triumphant at the end of combat. Well, it's more like two oddly shaped fighters slap away at each other, with odd physics providing hilarious comedy!

TIME LINE

2008 – LITTLEBIGPLANET
2009 – LITTLEBIGPLANET (PSP)
2010 – SACKBOY'S PREHISTORIC MOVES
2011 – LITTLEBIGPLANET 2
2012 – LITTLEBIGPLANET VITA
2012 – LITTLEBIGPLANET KARTING
2014 – RUN SACKBOY! RUN!
2014 – LITTLEBIGPLANET 3

ALSO CHECK OUT . . .

LITTLEBIGPLANET KARTING
This spin-off has more for those who want to create interesting and innovative racetracks.

PROJECT SPARK
Xbox One's interesting creation game isn't quite as cute as *LittleBigPlanet*, but it has just as much depth, and tons of tools to play with.

PIXELJUNK EDEN
If simple-to-play platformers with extremely unique graphics are your thing, definitely try *PixelJunk Eden* at some point.

METROID

NINTENDO'S ACTION STAR

Many years ago—back on the Nintendo Entertainment System—*Metroid* was something of a new idea. Here you had a world to explore, but you were blocked from accessing certain areas until you'd collected particular abilities. This genre of game soon became known as Metroidvania.

While there haven't been any new *Metroid* titles recently, Wii U owners can see what the fuss is about thanks to the recent release of *Metroid Prime Trilogy*, which packages *Metroid Prime*, *Metroid Prime 2: Echoes*, and *Metroid Prime 3: Corruption* together. Protagonist Samus Aran has been keeping busy, too, appearing in the recent *Super Smash Bros.* as both Samus and Zero Suit Samus. You can also play the original *Metroid* on 3DS!

DID YOU KNOW?

The password *JUSTIN BAILEY* for the original *Metroid* allowed you to play as Samus Aran without her Power Suit, wearing a pink leotard.

STATS

1.85 million sales, on average, per release

48 different abilities, upgrades, or alternate forms in the series

Average Metacritic score of **88.22**

12 *Metroid* games

TOP **5** BOSS BATTLES

PHANTOON

1 This ghostly boss first appears in *Super Metroid*, spitting slime and spectral fireballs at you. It's the second fight with him—in *Metroid: Other M*—that really excites, though. He's huge and tough to beat, and your battle with him leaves the arena devastated. This is a master class from Nintendo on how to design boss fights.

METROID PRIME

2 The fight with the main boss of *Metroid Prime* (yes, that is its name) is a staged one, requiring you first to quickly switch weapon types to deal out damage, then to use bombs to defeat its final form and the mini Metroids it brings with it.

RUNDAS

3 This guy begins *Metroid Prime 3: Corruption* as an ally of Samus and even helps her out from time to time. You're eventually forced to fight him, however, in a battle that has him zipping around the room with his Iceman-like frost powers. Not only is this tricky, but the cool (ha!) visual effects help this battle stand out.

META RIDLEY

4 Ridley is a regular boss in the *Metroid* series, and Samus's main rival. He pops up a number of times, but when you battle him—his upgraded and enhanced version—in *Metroid Prime*, it's a real test of your power and skills.

DARK SAMUS

5 Though there are a lot of similarities between Samus and Dark Samus, this is in fact a being of Phazon, the poisonous energy that appears throughout the *Metroid Prime* trilogy. This is a tough battle, since it's technically against yourself!

COMMENT

Grant Ball
"Treesicle" on YouTube

As a kid, I played *Metroid Prime* and *Metroid Fusion* religiously for what seems like years. Samus Aran (the protagonist) was the first character we covered on our YouTube channel for this very reason. As far as *Metroid*'s impact on the gaming community as a whole is concerned, I believe it brings a sense of perseverance and gritty exploration that players can apply to real-life situations and experiences. Each game, you must gain back your lost abilities, only to become even stronger than you were before. This sense of accomplishment becomes even greater thanks to the dark, foreboding atmospherics throughout the series that you must constantly outsmart and overcome.

ALSO CHECK OUT . . .

CASTLEVANIA

The "vania" part of *Metroidvania* comes from this series from Konami—that probably tells you quite a bit about how similar it is to *Metroid*.

GUACAMELEE!

This game takes the familiar *Metroid* format of themed "zones" and bosses and applies it to a very colorful Mexican wrestling theme.

ARKHAM ASYLUM

It has a small area to explore but a range of unlockable abilities and gadgets that you need for access: The comparison with *Metroid* is clear.

CIVILIZATION

WORLD IN YOUR HANDS

Civilization is one of the longest-running series in gaming, giving gamers a chance to build their own empires and conquer nations since 1991. Last year, *Civilization: Beyond Earth* let series fans take their adventures to space, where players shaped human advancement rather than civilizations and how they develop. You could even establish contact with an alien race! In the meantime, on iOS and Android, *Civilization Revolution 2* offered an easier version of the series to dive into. And for those who just want to sink their teeth into traditional strategy, there's *Civilization V: Complete Edition*, which comes with all the DLC. There's been plenty of choice this year for *Civilization* fans!

DID YOU KNOW?

Sid Meier is the original (and current) designer of the *Civilization* series, and the only developer to have his name on the front of the box.

STATS

94: the highest Metacritic rating for the series

81 different technologies to research in *Civilization V*

6,050 years in a full game

43 playable civilizations in the series

TOP  5 WORLD WONDERS

THE PYRAMIDS

1 This is a great Wonder to focus on early in the game, since the 25 percent upgrade to Worker production means that you can improve your cities and their resources quicker than anyone else can—and it gives you two free Workers to do it!

THE GREAT LIBRARY

2 This is another early Wonder that's good to get as soon as you can: It provides you with free technologies (very important), extra science resources, and even a free Library so you don't need to build one.

PETRA

3 Though this famous symbol of Jordan was added only in *Civilization 5*'s *Gods and Kings* expansion pack, it's still a great Wonder to get for your civilization. It transforms any desert city (which would be tough to grow and develop) into a paradise, even bringing extra culture resources with it!

NOTRE DAME

4 If you're the type of leader who likes to expand and conquer other civilizations using brute force, you'll really need to consider building Notre Dame. It's a huge boost to overall happiness in your cities, and it's very important once you start capturing cities to keep the residents happy and on your side.

LEANING TOWER OF PISA

5 Though the extra Great Person production is helpful, it's better to build this for the free Great Engineer it produces. This means that you can build another brand-new Wonder instantly, for free!

TIME LINE

1991	CIVILIZATION
1995	CIVNET
1996	CIVILIZATION II
1996	CIVILIZATION II: CONFLICTS IN CIVILIZATION
1997	CIVILIZATION II: FANTASTIC WORLDS
1999	CIVILIZATION II: TEST OF TIME
2001	CIVILIZATION III
2002	CIVILIZATION III: PLAY THE WORLD
2003	CIVILIZATION III: CONQUESTS
2005	CIVILIZATION IV
2006	CIVILIZATION IV: WARLORDS
2007	CIVILIZATION IV: BEYOND THE SWORD
2008	CIVILIZATION IV: COLONIZATION
2008	CIVILIZATION REVOLUTION
2010	CIVILIZATION V
2011	CIVILIZATION WORLD
2012	CIVILIZATION V: GODS AND KINGS
2013	CIVILIZATION V: BRAVE NEW WORLD
2014	CIVILIZATION REVOLUTION 2
2014	CIVILIZATION: BEYOND EARTH

ALSO CHECK OUT . . .

CIVILIZATION: BEYOND EARTH
This is almost the same *Civilization* experience, but it has a sci-fi twist. Now you're fighting aliens!

TOTAL WAR
This is similar . . . but when it comes to combat, it becomes completely different, requiring you to manage your units in real time on a battlefield.

ENDLESS LEGEND
If you want something a little more fantastical, then *Endless Legend* is for you. You can use all sorts of magic and monsters to decimate your foes.

BEST SOUNDTRACKS IN GAMING

BASTION

WHY: Supergiant Games' *Bastion* is a gem of an action game, and its soundtrack, composed by Darren Korb, is one of the biggest reasons for that. A fantastic mix of feisty guitar tunes, futuristic electronic tracks, and melancholy acoustic songs, it does a great job of mirroring *Bastion*'s story in audio form. It's a great listen on its own.

JOURNEY

WHY: *Journey* can be a lonely game at times. Anonymous companions join you only on occasion. But you're not really alone—you're joined by Austin Wintory's magnificent soundtrack. At times playful, at times heartbreaking, the music is a huge part of what makes *Journey*'s, well, journey so powerful and memorable.

FINAL FANTASY X

WHY: You could easily fill this list with nothing but *Final Fantasy*, but we're sticking to just one game here. Legendary composer Nobuo Uematsu worked with Masashi Hamauzu and Junya Nakano to create *Final Fantasy X*'s masterful score in 2001. The opening theme, "Zanarkand," still gives us chills.

ROCK BAND 3

WHY: We're cheating a bit with this one, but when it comes to the sheer number of awesome songs included in a game, *Rock Band 3* can't be beaten. The game comes with a killer set list of 83 classics, but where it truly shines is in its incredible selection of over 1,600 downloadable tracks.

VIVA PINATA

WHY: *Viva Piñata* from legendary games studio Rare was one of the most charming games on Xbox 360, and its adorable look was matched perfectly by Grant Kirkhope's beautiful soundtrack. It's calming, inspiring, uplifting, and relaxing to listen to!

SOUND SHAPES

WHY: Not only does the upbeat electronic soundtrack go hand in hand with the colorful platforming, it's a part of the actual game, too. Obstacles and enemies move in time to the music, so *Sound Shapes* feels like part puzzle game, part interactive album. It features excellent original music, too.

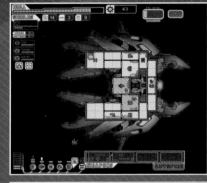

FTL: FASTER THAN LIGHT

WHY: We tend to associate games set in space with grand, cinematic scores, but *FTL: Faster Than Light* manages to buck the trend, setting the vast sprawl of the cosmos to a remarkably minimal soundtrack. It's a testament to the result that sometimes, in between exploring derelict space stations, discovering alien species, and fighting off pirate raids, we like to sit for a minute and enjoy the beautiful electronica.

HALO: THE MASTER CHIEF COLLECTION

WHY: *Dun dun dun duuhhnn, dun dun dun duuhhnn . . .* everyone knows how it goes! Nothing in gaming gets the blood pumping quite like the *Halo* theme. The legendary music has been through dozens of variations over the years, but it still packs a punch every single time players jump in a Warthog.

THE LEGEND OF ZELDA: THE WIND WAKER

WHY: The *Zelda* series has been famous for its music since the NES, but the *Wind Waker* soundtrack stands out as the finest of the series. From the jaunty flutes of its opening music to the rousing theme that plays whenever Link sets sail on the Great Sea, the score is packed full of memorable tunes.

SUPER MARIO GALAXY

WHY: You'd be hard-pressed to find somebody who isn't familiar with the *Super Mario* soundtrack: The iconic jingle is just as famous as the plumber's mustache and overalls. But while the tune has featured in countless *Mario* games through the years, the sweeping soundtrack of *Super Mario Galaxy* stands out. It's still recognizably *Mario*, but the addition of a 50-piece symphony orchestra adds an epic feel.

THE EXPERT SAYS . . .
GRANT KIRKHOPE
Award-winning composer for *Viva Piñata*, *Banjo-Kazooie*, and *Civilization: Beyond Earth*

I loved writing the score for *Viva Piñata*. The music of Elgar and Vaughan Williams kept running through my mind, that kind of archetypal English sound—I just thought that it suited the look and feel of the game. This was my first time using a live orchestra, and I really poured my heart and soul into this music. Of all the music I've written over the years, this is probably my favorite. "Bedtime Story" is definitely my favorite piece, followed closely by "Tranquil Hours."

DID YOU KNOW?

The original *Space Invaders* was the first-ever game to feature a continuous background soundtrack when it was released in 1978.

GAMING CLICHES WE ALL KNOW & LOVE

ZOMBIES!

WHY: From the truly scary zombies in horror games to the comedy ones that can be found in the likes of *Plants vs. Zombies*, these guys have shuffled their way out of the grave and into our hearts. Just keep them a safe distance away—they're likely to smell a bit, and they can often get a bit hungry and look for a fleshy snack . . .

LOTS OF BATS

WHY: If you're playing any kind of game that has a cave in it, you'll probably have to deal with bats—and you can be sure that those bats will be the most irritating enemy in the game. Bats are a pain no matter what you're playing, and you can understand why some people are scared of the dark!

THE WEAK SPOT

WHY: It's not easy to battle something that breathes fire and is at least three times your size. Luckily, most bosses very considerately wear great big signposts like red marks or weird eyes that let you know just how to take them down. These tend to prove very useful when you come up against a tricky foe.

AND NOW WE MUST BATTLE!

WHY: In some games, everything you do leads to battle. Meet a friend in a *Yu-Gi-Oh!* game? That's an obvious invitation to duel. Walk along the road in a *Pokémon* game? People will ask for a battle for no reason. Why can't we just get along?

Hunh? What do you think you're do What, you're going to protect him

THE MASHER

WHY: Nothing is more annoying than when you've practiced a game for ages, and then someone who has never played it beats you by randomly jabbing at buttons. But if you're on the other side of it, it sure is fun to show them up without any effort! Just try not to break the buttons on your controller.

SWEET SPOTS

WHY: No matter how cleverly the computer plays a game, we're still able to outsmart most AIs. Whether it's the perfect position to shoot from or a fighting combo that hits every time, once you uncover a sweet spot, it can be a lifesaver. But don't rely on it all the time—real people won't fall for it.

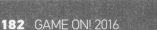

PERFECT ENDING

WHY: Sometimes you think you're closing in on the end of a game, since it feels like forever since you've seen or done anything new, and suddenly you'll receive a new weapon or power of some kind. Once that happens, you *know* it's nearly time for the credits to roll. Worse yet, you'll probably only ever get to use that power in the final showdown. Talk about saving the best for last . . .

EVERYONE HAS GILLS

WHY: How many times have you taken your favorite characters underwater? And how many times have they *not* had trouble breathing? Mario seems so happy spending long stretches under the sea that we think he might be half-plumber, half-fish. And come to think of it, if he is, then most of his friends who follow him down must be, too . . . On top of that, you never see them drying their clothes.

SUSPICIOUS SAVE POINT

WHY: If you should come across a big, scary-looking door with a save point next to it, it's best to use the point—there's most likely a boss fight about to happen. If you find lots of pickups in the same place, it's almost certain that you're going to have to battle something big. Even experienced gamers sometimes fail to recognize these warning signs, but the quicker you learn them, the easier things get.

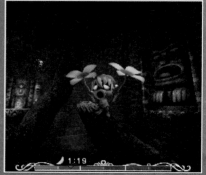

NEW BEGINNINGS

WHY: A sequel has been announced. Hooray! But wait a minute—won't this be a bit easy? After all, the hero collected tons of brilliant equipment and learned some really awesome moves in the last game. Don't worry—they'll change the hero, or make something terrible happen to him, or even pretend that the last game didn't really exist, and either way you'll be starting from scratch.

THE EXPERT SAYS . . .
CHRISTOPHER FOLTZ
"Chrisandthemike" on YouTube

THE BOSS (METAL GEAR)

My favorite gaming cliché is an antagonist that can actually be interpreted as not only a bad guy, but a good guy, too. There are two sides to every video-game story, and this is what drives me to continue whatever objectives are thrown at me. When a video game dives into the backstory of the main villain, I am driven to find out more. They have been preventing me from completing my quest. I love to find out why they want to stop me. My favorite gaming cliché? There are two sides to every story.

JECHT (FINAL FANTASY X)

BATTLEBORN
GAMING'S BIGGEST GENRES COLLIDE

What happens when you cross FPS games with MOBAs? *Battleborn* is the answer! This colorful project is being made by Gearbox Software, creators of *Borderlands*, so you can be assured this will be incredible when it's released later this year!

THE COOLEST GAMING SECRETS OF ALL TIME

THE COOLEST GAMING SECRETS OF ALL TIME

SUPER MARIO 64
DINO CRISIS

Mario fans were understandably a little disappointed to say good-bye to Yoshi after his excellent work in the SNES games . . . or at least they were until they managed to round up all 120 Stars. Upon reaching 100 percent completion, a cannon unlocks in the castle grounds and fires our hero right up onto the roof, where our green friend (no, not Luigi) is waiting. Sadly, you can't ride him this time, but he will chuck you a bunch of 1-Ups. It's a bit late for that, buddy!

DID YOU KNOW?

The secret rooms in *Portal* and *Portal 2* belong to Doug Rattmann, a former Aperture scientist, who became a little unhinged.

BRAID
STAR POWER

Thought you were smart for solving all of *Braid*'s brain-twisting puzzles, did you? Think again. In addition to all the puzzle pieces to round up, there are also eight secret Stars to find, and they're annoyingly well hidden. We're not going to spoil any of the solutions or locations, but you'll need to do a lot of experimenting, skilled platforming, and even waiting around if you want to find them all. Is your brain up to the challenge?

I'm sorry, but the Princess is in another castle.

SHENMUE II
UNDERGROUND DUCK RACING

To get involved in supersecret duck stuff, you first need to deliberately fail the QTE in the Lai Lai Eatery. Talk to the waitress afterward, and you'll get a Bronze Medal. You can now go to the third floor of the arcade, where you need to beat Eileen and Izumi for a Silver Medal. Now head to the Tomato Mart and talk to Izumi. Once you win a duck race, go to the red tree where you catch leaves and keep doing that until you get a duck. Now you can train your duck up; win a race with your duck for a Gold Medal.

FINAL FANTASY VII
SEE AERIS'S GHOST

So we all know that once Aeris dies, she's gone for good. Nothing is going to bring her back to life once that tear-jerking moment has happened. But you *can* see her ghost in the Church in Midgar later in the game. Once you get the Airship and can travel the world at your leisure, go to Midgar and speak to the guy there. Then head to Bone Village. Have the villagers look for Normal Treasure, and keep them at it until you get the Key to Sector 5 (from the very start of the game, make sure everyone has All Materia equipped all the time, as once they're maxed out you can sell one for a lot of Gil). Go back to Midgar, and the key will open the door. This is a onetime deal, so keep your eyes peeled the moment you step into the Church, and you will catch a flash of Aeris's ghost tending the flowers with the children. Premium Heart can also be found here.

MIRROR'S EDGE
SURPRISE GIANT RAT

Rats are kind of a thing in *Mirror's Edge* (it was a weird in-joke at DICE). On Part D of the level Kate, you can make a giant rat just appear out of nowhere and go running down the street. And we're talking the size of a car. If you want to catch sight of this speedy creature, zoom in to where there are nine white dots on orange. Wait for the truck to come around the corner, shoot it in the engine, then shoot the middle of those three dots.

PES 6
OSTRICHES VS. DINOSAURS?

Soccer's pretty popular, right? We hear those *FIFA* and *PES* games sell pretty darn well. But for all the thrill of the beautiful game, sometimes it just feels like it needs a little something extra. Like all the players on one team becoming enormous penguins, while the opposition rides dinosaurs. Or ostriches. Well, in *PES 6* you can make that happen! Just buy the Ostrich, Raptor, or Penguin costume, change it before the match, and you and your friends are in for an excellent time.

THE COOLEST GAMING SECRETS OF ALL TIME

DID YOU KNOW?

Celebrate a victory in *FIFA 14* and do the "Gangnam Style" dance by unlocking the Celebration "Gallop Dance."

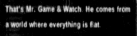

That's Mr. Game & Watch. He comes from a world where everything is flat.

SUPER SMASH BROS. BRAWL
CODEC YOUR BUDDIES

Metal Gear is so awesome that its awesomeness has spilled over into a bunch of other games. One of the things you can do in *Smash Bros. Brawl*, if you play as Snake on his Shadow Moses level, is call up your buddies, like Otacon and Mei Ling, and get specific info on the characters you can battle in *Smash Bros. Melee*. Just do a really quick down taunt and you should receive a Codec call with some helpful (and not-so-helpful) info on who you're fighting.

LEGO THE HOBBIT
EVERYBODY DANCE NOW

Yep, you can get magic boots that make your buddies dance with you. Just go to the Rivendell statue, following the studs to a door marked "H," jumping up the bouncy ropes, pulling the lever on the way and the one at the top. When on the ground again, jump up those handholds, pull *that* lever, and the Schematic for Mithril Dance Boots will be revealed. Forge them in the Blacksmith's shop in Bree once you've completed the Smithy In Peril quest.

Total Time 1' 13" 172

Time 16 START

Lap Time 1' 13" 172 Ghost 0' 56" 947

OUTRUN 2
BREAK-DANCING FLAG GUY

Okay, the race has started! Go! Drive! Or . . . or not? While you *should* be putting pedal to the metal and tearing rubber off the tracks, you might want to try staying at the starting position for just a moment. It takes around 20 seconds, but just wait and watch. The flag-waving guy at the start of the race will get bored and do a little break dancing. Watch him bust out some sweet moves before you run out of time.

THE LEGEND OF ZELDA: A LINK TO THE PAST
HIDDEN GEM ROOM

Nintendo held a competition way back in 1990, and the winner's name was supposed to make a cameo in a mystery NES game. While the winner, Chris Houlihan, didn't actually get his name in an NES game, he did get a hard-to-find secret room in *A Link to the Past*—called the Top Secret Room, or Chris Houlihan's Room—named after him. It's theorized that this room was created as a kind of fail-safe, should the game experience an error condition while loading a screen, so the best way to get to this room is to try to confuse the game. One option that frequently works is loading up a save from the Sanctuary, dashing left, down, and up around to the secret entrance under the bush that takes you to Hyrule Castle, the one on the right side of the Castle itself. You have to dash there, making the game work extra hard to keep up with you so that it glitches you out into the Top Secret Room. Once you're in the room, you'll find a great bonus of 45 blue rupees, and a message: "My name is Chris Houlihan. This is my top secret room. Keep it between us, OK?"

RESOGUN
CRAZY-DIFFICULT CHALLENGE

So let's say you're pretty good at *Resogun*. You've completed all ten levels on all the difficulties you can see—time to kick back and chase high scores, right? Nope! There's an extra, hidden difficulty level—Master—that doesn't show up anywhere in the game until you've unlocked it. There are no hints about it, either; you just have to complete Arcade mode on Veteran. You *also* have to do it solo, with no multiplayer help. Eek.

BATMAN: ARKHAM ASYLUM
ARKHAM CITY BLUEPRINTS

Despite being out two years before *Arkham City*, *Arkham Asylum* actually contains a hidden room in which you can see the map of the city itself on the walls, with "Approved" stamped on it. For the puzzle solvers who found all of the Riddler's secrets, this awesome hint to the next game was a brilliant find. Blow up the plain five-paneled wall in Warden Sharp's office with explosive gel to take a look.

NBA JAM BIG HEAD MODE

NBA Jam has a ton of unlockable stuff, but our favorite definitely has to be Big Head Mode (and it does exactly what you'd expect!). This ridiculously stupid/fun mode was originally in the 1993 arcade game—hold down Up, Turbo, and Steal from the Tonight's Matchup screen to the tip-off—but it was also kept in for other versions, including 2010's Wii version seen here, where you can get it by finishing Jam Camp mode.

TEKKEN 6
ITEM MOVES

Character customization has been a part of the *Tekken* series for some time now; here, some special items were added that actually grant the wearer access to some cool new moves. Some of the ones added later for *Tekken Tag Tournament 2* are universal and work with every character, but it's with the unique personal items that the real fun lies. Kuma can wear a tutu to get a ballerina pirouette; Paul can make his hair grow taller at will; Lili has a pair of magic shorts that can summon baby penguins (yes, really); Anna can kick her shoe off to hit opponents . . . The list goes on. They don't do a lot of damage (if any), but they're pretty much all good for a giggle.

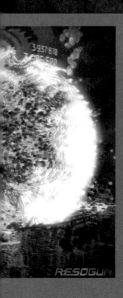

THE COOLEST GAMING SECRETS OF ALL TIME

DESTINY
BUNGIE'S SOCCER MADNESS

It was in *Halo 2* that gamers originally found a random ball on certain levels, assumed to be a leftover physics test. They found that a lot of fun could be had with it, with players even assigning landmarks as goalposts to get a real game in. Because it was so well received, secret soccer balls have been in lots of *Halo* games since, and one can even be found in the new *Destiny*, on the crates in the Tower hub.

THE MANY USES OF THE KONAMI CODE

Up, up, down, down, left, right, left, right, B, A. Probably the most famous cheat code in history, the Konami Code first appeared in the old-school shooter *Gradius*, but it has made *hundreds* of appearances since. Most Konami games use it in some way, whether as a proper cheat code or as a retro reference, but its cultural impact is even bigger—countless other games use the famous code (or a variant of it) to activate cheat modes and Easter eggs. Such is the impact of this set of inputs that it has even been coded into various websites to trigger secret pages, messages, and oddities that you wouldn't otherwise see. Remember it well, for this one cheat code will never die and could lead you to all manner of cool secrets. Go try it out today!

TONY HAWK'S PRO SKATER 2
BECOME SPIDER-MAN

Tony Hawk games have always had a great sense of fun to them, and what's more fun than being able to play as your friendly neighborhood Spider-Man? To get Spider-Man as a playable character, you need to create your own skater to play with and then get 100 percent in Career Mode. It sounds pretty simple, but this can take some time. Spider-Man also comes with four alternative costumes, including a supercool Venom one.

THE COOLEST GAMING SECRETS OF ALL TIME

MEGA MAN X
HADOUKEN!

While it's a bit of a chore to get, it's worth it for one-hit KOs (although it doesn't stick around when you save). Get yourself a bunch of extra lives (ideally the full nine), beat all eight bosses, and have all the upgrades. On the moving platform section, when it starts to dip, jump up to the ledge with the Energy Capsule, then jump off again to the left. Do this four times, and Dr. Light will appear to give it to you.

MARIO KART 8
BEAT THE BLUE SHELL

Yes, that's right, you can actually avoid this nightmare of a power-up and keep your lead, but doing so will take a little skill. The horn is the easiest way to prevent a blue shell from ruining your chances of winning, but other items work too—the star (which makes you invincible) and Bullet Bill both save your skin if you can hold them all the way to first place, and even the lowly mushroom can do the trick. Time your boost just as the shell is about to land and you'll escape the blast!

POKÉMON
HIDDEN STATS

Not all Pokémon are created equal, and there's a lot going on behind the scenes that the series is only now starting to make a little more visible. Hidden stats come in two flavors— IVs (Individual Values) and EVs (Effort Values). IVs are created on your first encounter with a monster, a number from 0 to 31 assigned to each stat to determine its maximum possible value. EVs, on the other hand, are earned by defeating other monsters in battle, with a maximum of 252 per stat and 510 overall. With this knowledge, you can manipulate stat growth as you train your Pokémon, and it isn't just EVs that can be modified—advanced breeding techniques in more recent games allow you to keep hatching eggs until you find the perfect companion. This blew our minds when we first heard about it, and it makes a big difference. Super Training in the new games is basically just a new way to boost EVs through minigames—battle a lot with a particular monster and you'll notice that its graph grows without even touching the tedious minigames. Master this mechanic and you'll soon have the most powerful team possible!

THE COOLEST GAMING SECRETS OF ALL TIME

SPELUNKY
MYSTERIOUS CITIES OF GOLD

The randomly generated caverns of *Spelunky* are basically one big secret, but there are several constants should you get good enough to survive the descent. First, find the Udjat Eye in a chest in the Mines. This will lead to the Black Market in the Jungle, where you can buy the Ankh for $50,000. Then find the Moai statue in the Ice Caves and die—you'll respawn inside the Moai (thanks, Ankh!) and can grab the Hedjet. Finally, defeat the powerful Anubis in the first Temple stage to grab his Scepter. Doing all this makes a gold door appear in 4-2, taking you to your destination: a level made of pure gold where you'll become superrich! Well, if you survive . . .

PORTAL 2
TURRET BARBERSHOP QUARTET

Okay, this one's a little complicated. In Test Chamber 16, go past the turret in the vent past the elevator. Use portals on the single turret's laser to blow up the group of them, then use the Refraction Cube to aim the robot's laser at itself. When the grate explodes, head on through. A lot of pretty dark things happened here in this world that Chell now lives in, but this hidden barbershop quartet of turrets is somehow one of the creepiest secrets. Just listen to it— you'll see what we mean. The vent also features mysterious scribblings from Doug Rattmann, so keep an eye out for those, too.

Once again, my brother went on an exciting journey.

PAPER MARIO
LUIGI'S SAD DIARY

Poor Luigi. While he's come into his own a little with the *Luigi's Mansion* series, we always suspected he felt like the underappreciated sibling to his considerably more famous brother. Hidden in the basement of their house—head to the weird-looking floorboard to the far left and use the ground pound you get in Chapter Three—are various sad, weird diary entries from the green-suited, green-eyed guy. "So unfair!"

TEKKEN 3
FARTING FIERY DINOSAUR

Along with Doctor Bosconovitch, Gon is one of two unlockable playable characters in *Tekken 3*. This cute little guy can be unlocked once you've beaten him in *Tekken Ball*—and you can unlock *that* by defeating Ogre. Alternatively, you can unlock him by getting a high score in Survival Mode and entering "GON." Gon has his own Japanese TV series and manga; he's actually way more famous than just being a little dinosaur in *Tekken*.

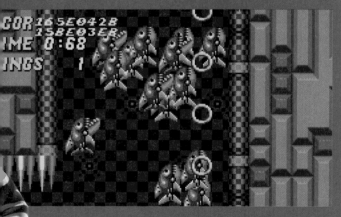

SONIC 2
MY FIRST LEVEL EDITOR

By playing songs in the sound-test menu in order to spell out the game's release date (1, 9, 9, 2, 1, 1, 2, 4—November 24, 1992), it's possible to tinker with the layout of the levels by placing new objects, enemies, and gimmicks however you like. It's a little fiddly, but still a lot of fun to mess around with, allowing you to create your own obstacle courses or spawn helpful items at will. A similar feature even existed in the original game, but it was present only in the first run of cartridges produced. What kinds of cool things will you make?

SUPER MARIO WORLD
STAR WORLD SPEED RUN

Widely regarded as one of the best games ever made, *Super Mario World* is a true platforming classic, and one that doesn't skimp when it comes to cool secrets. One of the best of the bunch is Star World, accessed only by finding a hidden exit in one of five of the game's main stages. Each leads to a different Star World stage, meaning that, in theory, you would have to find all five secret portals to do them all. Cunningly, though, the Star World levels have their own hidden exits, and finding one allows you to link up all the Star World stages and effectively warp around the game. The biggest impact of this is that with a little skill, it's possible to beat the game in under ten minutes, clearing just 12 of the game's 73 levels. Head to Donut Secret Ghost House in World 2 and find the hidden exit there to unlock Star Road. Then, by finding the secret exits in the first four Star World stages, you'll be able to warp back down to the surface and will find yourself right outside Bowser's fortress! Your skills will be tested here, but no more than along the way . . .

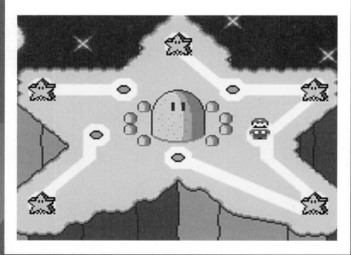

FINAL FANTASY XII
THE ZODIAC SPEAR

Like rare weapons? Then you're going to love this. The ultimate weapon is near impossible to obtain without a guide, since it appears only if you don't open a selection of chests in the rest of the game. There is another way to get it, but it's even more ridiculous, and the drop rate is horribly low. There's just a 10 percent chance of a chest appearing, then a 10 percent chance of it holding anything, then a 10 percent chance of it being the Zodiac Spear. A 0.1 percent chance. We don't like those odds . . .

SECRET THAT STAYED HIDDEN THE LONGEST
FINAL FANTASY IX
NERO FAMILY SIDE QUEST

We're going to throw out a nod to the *Final Fantasy* series as a whole for having some great secrets and hidden things to find (seriously, *FFVIII*, an alien called Pupu?). Despite it being in the official Japanese guides, Western gamers didn't discover this quest line for 13 years. It's no *FFXII* Zodiac Spear side quest, that's for sure, as it basically only involves repeatedly returning to the Tantalus hideout from the start of disc four and speaking to members of the Nero family, who keep losing other family members. Keep playing the main quest, but if you return and talk to them enough, the family gets back together, and you'll be rewarded with a Protect Ring from the chest.

FEZ
MYSTERIOUS OWL PARLIAMENT

Fez is basically made of secrets. What are those cubes? How can you decode that weird language? (Hint: Pay attention to the animals.) And why are there all those owls everywhere? Amid all of *Fez*'s easy, not-so-easy, and downright evil puzzles, finding all four owls gets you not only a cubelet but also an anti-cube and weird conversations with each mystical owl. Check out the walls of eyepatch-wearing Geezer's home for where to find them all.

od job! You finished the hardest
rsion of the game! This is the
velopment room for the Chrono
gger game.

CHRONO TRIGGER
MEET THE DEVELOPERS

This excellent SNES RPG from Square has a bunch of different endings you can get, but if you defeat Lavos—an alien parasite and *Chrono Trigger*'s big bad—at the start of the game, you'll end up at the End of Time, where you can speak to all the game's developers. Our favorite is Yoshinori Kitase, (appearing as the little cat Alfador), who asks you if you got through all ten different endings and gives you the tip that they all depend on when you challenge Lavos.

DID YOU KNOW?

In *The Sims 3*, if you use the Time Machine, there are tons of references to other games like *Mass Effect*.

GOLDENEYE 007
HIDDEN SPECTRUM GAMES

GoldenEye 007 is notorious for its secrets, but its most hidden secret by far is something that isn't even in the game at all, but rather in its coding. To test out whether it was possible, the devs ran a ZX Spectrum emulator through it, then just disabled it before launch. But! With the use of a downloadable patch and an N64 emulator to play *GoldenEye 007* itself (so many emulators), these rare retro classics can be discovered.

X-MEN ORIGINS: WOLVERINE
NOT A LIE

We're suckers for a good *Portal* reference. Sure, you can bake a cake in *Minecraft* or *World of Warcraft* to unlock the achievements The Lie and The Cake Is Not a Lie respectively, but in *X-Men Origins: Wolverine*'s secrets there *actually is cake*. And players don't even have to make it themselves—in the freeze ray room, they just move the teleporter as far to the right as it will go and teleport themselves there. It makes up for GLaDOS's empty promises . . .

SELECT YOUR CRAFT

NABOO STARFIGHTER
SECONDARY WEAPON: SEEKER TORPEDOES

STAR WARS: ROGUE SQUADRON
SECRET NABOO STARFIGHTER

So what do you do when you've got a *Star Wars* game coming out, and there's a new *Star Wars* movie for the first time in 15 years? Well, if you're anything like developer Factor 5, you work with LucasArts and make sure there's one of the cool new ships in your game. But there's a problem: Your game is releasing six months before the movie. Obviously you can't reveal such a spoiler for the film so far in advance, but what you can do—and whether you're a *Star Wars* fan or not, this is amazing—is hide it in the game's code anyway. You also need to swear your team to secrecy (those that even know about it in the first place, that is), and make sure it's so well hidden that not even a GameShark can find it. Months later, LucasArts revealed the code to unlock it as a playable ship: Go to Passcodes and enter CDYXF!?Q; when it resets, enter ASEPONE! The gaming world was stunned.

TERRARIA
DRESS LIKE LINK

As one of several little nods to one of *Terraria*'s RPG inspirations, you can make a certain Triforce-seeking, Master Sword–wielding "Hero's Clothes" tribute outfit to go adventuring in. The Hero's Hat, Hero's Shirt, and Hero's Pants each cost 3 Green Thread and 20 Silk, so you need 420 Cobwebs (just save them up when you come across a Spider Nest) and 27 Jungle Grass Seeds (cut down grass in the jungle for these rare, random drops).

THE COOLEST GAMING SECRETS OF ALL TIME

NINTENDO GAMECUBE
ODD NOISES

We've talked about a bunch of games— now how about a secret that is actually built into a console? The famous GameCube start-up jingle is actually one of three possible variants, though we're not quite sure how anyone found out about the other two or why they even exist. Hold the Z button on one controller as you hit the power button, and you'll hear squeaks, boings, and giggles in place of the regular melody, or hold Z on four connected controllers to get drums, bells, and wood blocks.

The time has come to tell you some of my secrets.

DID YOU KNOW?

Taunts in *Street Fighter III* aren't just for show—they all have unique perks as well. Try them all out to see what they do!

ILLUSION OF TIME
WEIRD SECRET LEVEL

Illusion of Time has a great, if completely unrewarded, secret: Find 50 hidden/invisible Red Jewels throughout the game and you get to play a secret beastie-filled area. The worst one to get is from the South Cape fisherman. After you're done playing with your friends, go in and out of the hideout until a fisherman appears, looking off to the right. Speak to him for a Red Jewel. When you have 50 at the Tower of Babel, return to Dao and speak to Jeweler Gem.

THE EXPERT SAYS . . .
"LAURENZSIDE"
YouTuber

The one secret that comes to mind is finding Mew in *Pokémon Yellow Version*. Mew is my all-time favorite Pokémon, so not being able to really have it available in the games was heartbreaking. My older cousin was always coming to me with *Pokémon* game "tricks" he had heard about from friends that we should try. I was about ten years old when *Pokémon Yellow Version* came out, and *again* my cousin eventually came to me with a new way to catch Mew. In short, catch an Abra, walk superclose to the (unfought) Trainer on the left of Nugget Bridge, quickly teleport away with Abra before the battle begins, fight the first Trainer in Misty's Gym, then return to Nugget Bridge. Your Start Menu should pop up, press B . . . MEW!

SHADOW OF THE COLOSSUS
THE SECRET GARDEN

Serious spoilers ahead! The courtyard garden at the end of the game is actually accessible much earlier. At the base of the temple, find the moss that you can climb straight up until you come to the ledges, then always head to the right. You will need a *lot* of stamina for this. Keep going up the moss and right on the ledges until you come across the stairs. Now you can explore and eat a delicious stamina/health-decreasing piece of fruit . . . aww.

MOST INNOVATIVE GAMES

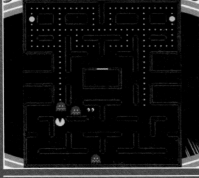

PAC-MAN

WHY: *Pac-Man* was the gateway to gaming for an entire generation. While the graphics and gameplay might not look so great by today's standards, in the '80s, *Pac-Man* was on the cutting edge! Best of all, the game's charming puzzle premise and simple controls meant that almost anyone could give it a try.

GUITAR HERO

WHY: There are some who may have hung up their plastic guitars and folded away their mics . . . but not us! Yes, the series became a tad bloated, but few games rock our world like *Guitar Hero*. Spawning a raft of similar music games, *Guitar Hero* was the one that had us all rocking out with friends.

WII SPORTS

WHY: Remember when motion control was a brand new sensation? Yup, that's why *Wii Sports* is on this list. Selling over 80 million copies and instantly making gaming accessible for all, *Wii Sports* is the reason why our parents can't complain that playing video games makes us fat!

ANGRY BIRDS

WHY: You might not want to admit it, but *Angry Birds* is still one of gaming's biggest sensations. Insanely successful and generating a host of sequels, merchandise, and copycat games, its bright colors, simple gameplay, and physics-based puzzles keep everyone coming back for more.

PORTAL

WHY: Even though the only gun we have doesn't fire bullets—and there's only a handful of characters in the entire game—*Portal*'s blend of perfect puzzles and crazy characters made it the surprise hit of 2007. Even now, it continues to entertain thanks to its wholly original puzzles and wonderfully funny story line.

LEGO GAMES

WHY: The *LEGO* franchise puts fun well and truly at the core of all its games. Never taking itself too seriously, the series has gone from strength to strength, offering fantastic co-op fun, top story lines, and a ton of crazy collectibles. Best of all, fans of *Batman*, *Harry Potter*, and the like had a riot!

MINECRAFT

WHY: The genius of *Minecraft* is that practically anything—and we do mean pretty much anything—is possible. It has amassed a huge cult following, and it's easy to see why the game is so popular, thanks to its unique charm, cooperative play, accessibility, and simple premise. Available on practically every platform you can imagine—from consoles to PCs to mobile phones—you can pick up and play any time, and have some serious fun doing it.

TEARAWAY

WHY: No game had really capitalized on the PlayStation Vita's exceptional touch-screen system until *Tearaway* came along. Offering a rich, vibrant experience that was not only engaging but also fully interactive, *Tearaway*'s cutesy, crafty world is one of the most exciting we've seen on handheld devices. Only by interacting with the screens and helping the messenger along can "the You" help puzzle out the secrets and complete the game!

SKYLANDERS

WHY: The first franchise to introduce real-life characters and a magical Portal of Power, *Skylanders* pushed the envelope when it came to developing cute, animated characters that employ their own unique spin on combat. Though *Disney Infinity* has done a wonderful job of capturing the essence of our favorite Disney characters, there's just something special about *Skylanders* and its original take on toys coming to life!

SUPER MARIO 3D WORLD

WHY: There's something about *Mario*'s pixel-perfect universe that makes almost every game a surefire success. Yet when it comes to *Super Mario 3D World*, it was the Wii U's game pad that became the star of the show. You'll need to think more creatively, paying special attention to your game pad, using all aspects of the device to progress.

THE EXPERT SAYS . . .
YOUTUBER "HEYCHRISSA"
Adventure games expert

LEGO GAMES

As a 27-year-old, I can proudly say that the *LEGO* games are up there with my top gaming experiences. Their ability to create fun gameplay that isn't difficult to master, the opportunity to follow along with some of your favorite stories and characters, the straightforward collect-and-build mechanics, the colorful graphics, and the comical and witty cut scenes make them enjoyable for people of all ages. There's something for everyone with *LEGO* games, and the pick-up-and-play aspect, plus the cooperative feature, offers an easy way for family and friends to play and enjoy the experience together.

PORTAL

GRAVITY-BUSTING FUN

We can't help thinking we would've have paid just a little bit more attention to science in school if it had been delivered by the people behind Aperture Science. In fact, it would've been our favorite class by far . . . even more than computer class or PE.

Playing as tight-lipped Chell, you're at the mercy of the menacing—but inexplicably awesome—GLaDOS, trying to outsmart your way to freedom as you methodically work your way through Aperture's insane puzzle asylum with your brains and Portal gun.

Portal 2 has been brought to more systems in the past year, and you can now play it on Linux and SteamOS, while co-op has been added to the Perpetual Testing Initiative, allowing you to create your own fiendish *Portal* puzzles!

DID YOU KNOW?

Writer Erik Wolpaw has confirmed that although lead character Chell actually can talk, she simply chooses not to.

STATS

GLaDOS
is short for *Genetic Lifeform and Disk Operating System*

Portal has a **90** **on Metacritic**

Portal 2 has a **95** **on Metacritic**

Portal 2 has won numerous awards, including **ULTIMATE GAME OF THE YEAR** at the 2011 Golden Joystick Awards

Portal had a development team of fewer than **10 people**

Portal 2 had a team of **30-40** people

TOP **5** GLADOS QUOTES

THINGS ARE GETTING PERSONAL

1 "Well done. Here are the test results: You are a horrible person. I'm serious, that's what it says: 'a horrible person.' We weren't even testing for that."

JUMPSUIT FASHION ADVICE

2 "You look ugly in that jumpsuit. That's not my opinion; it's right here on your fact sheet. They said on everyone else it looked fine, but on you, it looked hideous."

SMELLY GARBAGE

3 "Remember before when I was talking about smelly garbage standing around and being useless? That was a metaphor. I was actually talking about you. I'm sorry. You didn't react at the time, so I was worried it sailed right over your head."

SUPER SARCASM

4 "When I said 'deadly neurotoxin,' the 'deadly' was in massive sarcasm quotes. I could take a bath in this stuff. Put it on cereal, rub it right into my eyes. Honestly, it's not deadly at all . . . to me."

HOW TO CAPTURE YOUR SWORN ENEMIES

5 "If I'd known you'd let yourself get captured this easily, I'd have just dangled a turkey leg from the ceiling!"

TIME LINE

2007 – PORTAL

2011 – PORTAL 2

ALSO CHECK OUT . . .

TAG: THE POWER OF PAINT
Developed for Windows in 2009, this game inspired *Portal 2*'s paint mechanics.

A BOY AND HIS BLOB
Jump on your Wii and work with your pet blob to solve these brain-boggling puzzles.

ANTICHAMBER
This first-person puzzle platform game challenges you to think differently. Brace yourself for frustration, though!

NO MAN'S SKY

In every sense of the word, *No Man's Sky* has become the biggest indie game on console. Not only has Sony given its backing to this intriguing space exploration game, but the actual scale of it is enormous. Developer Hello Games thinks it will take 5 billion years to fully explore everything in it!

What's so interesting about *No Man's Sky* is that while combat is part of the game, that doesn't look to be the main focus. Instead, it's about discovering wildlife, seeing new creatures, and learning about the massive universe around you.

The overall goal is to reach the center of the galaxy, which takes between 40 and 100 hours. But *No Man's Sky* looks like it'll be about taking your time and getting immersed in a gorgeous world with plenty of depth . . .

DID YOU KNOW?

The universe is procedurally generated, which means that it is created by a computer code that generates the planets and creatures.

STATS

585 billion years: how long it'd take to find every planet

It could take up to **100** hours to reach the center of the universe

The code used to generate the universe is  **64** characters long

There are  **18** quintillion planets in the universe

TOP **5** SPACE MONSTERS

DIPLODOCUS

1 Though this doesn't necessarily look like the long-necked dinosaur we've all come to know and love, it is very similar in a lot of ways. Whether this thing will be a vegetarian like its Earth equivalent, we're not sure—you'll have to find out yourself. That's all part of the fun of discovery in *No Man's Sky*!

LAND WORM

2 These things are terrifying, and one thing's for certain—you don't want to get caught in the path of one of these giant land worms. They burrow around the planets that they are found on, appearing on the surface every so often. Judging by their size and how scaly they are, it might be worth avoiding them . . .

FLYING FISH

3 There are plenty of airborne creatures roaming the skies in *No Man's Sky*, and this interesting-looking animal is probably one of the most intriguing ones. Its tail flickers in the wind as though it's swimming through the air, and it's so big that it'll destroy any birds that dare attack it.

STEGOSAURUS

4 Okay, so this is the second dinosaur on this list, but hey, dinosaurs are cool, right?! This guy tends to be a little more aggressive than the previously mentioned diplodocus, though, so you don't want to stumble across a stampeding herd like this one!

ALSO CHECK OUT . . .

ELITE: DANGEROUS
This is a bit more serious, but if you're more interested in "realistic" sci-fi, then it might be an option for you.

THIS THING

5 Now this is a beast we've never seen before, and we're not quite sure what to call it. It does resemble a raptor—yes, even more dinosaur-like creatures—but it doesn't have any arms! It's pretty big, too, so you probably wouldn't have much chance of escaping it—look at the size of those legs!

STAR WARS: THE OLD REPUBLIC
This one doesn't play much like *No Man's Sky*, but there's battling bad guys and exploring galaxies here, too.

KINGDOM COME: DELIVERANCE
Instead of space and lasers, *Deliverance* has swords and shields. It's a realistic look at medieval life.

INDIE GAMES: BEST OF THE REST

INDIE GAMES: BEST OF THE REST

While they don't have huge development budgets, nothing can slow down the unstoppable spirit of indie games—the likes of *Spelunky* and *Fez* are now being played by millions of people the world over. There are loads of absolute gems made by small teams, with games such as *Rogue Legacy*, *The Swapper*, *Super Meat Boy*, and *Gang Beasts* offering hours of entertainment. Each of these celebrates a side of gaming that's often forgotten these days, with *Rogue Legacy* harking back to the side-scrolling platformer, while *Gang Beasts* allows you to have a pro wrestling match with lumps of clay. You'll have a great time with indie games, as they are often fun, simple, and easy to play!

DID YOU KNOW?

Rogue Legacy was made by brothers Kenny and Teddy Lee. It took them 18 months to develop, and they made their money back within an hour of release.

STATS

Average score for *The Swapper* (on PC):

87
on Metacritic

Super Meat Boy has sold over

1
million copies

Only

3
people worked on *Gang Beasts*

Rogue Legacy was produced on just a

$15k
budget

TOP 5 BEST INDIE GAMES

ROGUE LEGACY

1 A 2-D side-scrolling platformer, *Rogue Legacy* tasks you with killing five bosses in the randomly generated dungeons of a castle. With ever-increasing difficulty, it's designed to kill you over and over so that you learn how to get better at the game.

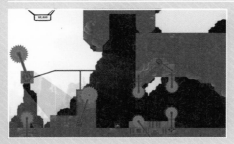

SUPER MEAT BOY

2 *Super Meat Boy* is hard. With over 300 levels that continually get tougher as you progress, it requires an incredible amount of patience and skill to complete. It's also fiendishly addictive and utterly entertaining. Don't miss it.

THE SWAPPER

3 Trapped on a ship in space, you're given the power to clone yourself and "swap" into different versions of your character in order to try to solve a series of puzzles. While simple to pick up and play, *The Swapper* has hidden depths.

GANG BEASTS

4 Two blobs of clay. One stage. Countless ways to kill your opponent. *Gang Beasts* was so popular even before it was released that a demo attracted a huge following from gamers all over the world. Get the gang together for local multiplayer fun.

NEVER ALONE

5 This gorgeous platforming game has you play as a young girl and her arctic fox, and it feels more like an interactive folktale. With beautiful storytelling and some tricky puzzles, *Never Alone* is a wonderful game to experience.

TIME LINE

2008 – CASTLE CRASHERS
2008 – BRAID
2008 – SPELUNKY
2009 – MINECRAFT
2010 – THOMAS WAS ALONE
2010 – LIMBO
2010 – SUPER MEAT BOY
2011 – THE BINDING OF ISAAC
2011 – BASTION
2012 – FEZ
2012 – HOTLINE MIAMI
2013 – DAY Z
2013 – TOWERFALL
2013 – THE SWAPPER
2013 – GONE HOME
2013 – DON'T STARVE
2013 – ROGUE LEGACY
2014 – TRANSISTOR
2014 – GANG BEASTS

ALSO CHECK OUT . . .

FIVE NIGHTS AT FREDDY'S

A game featuring stuffed toys and security cameras shouldn't be terrifying, but *Five Nights at Freddy's* proves that it can be. An indie fright fest, it will scare the stuffing out of those who play it.

GUACAMELEE!

Everyone loves a *luchador*, right? Based on Mexican folklore, *Guacamelee!* is an action platformer that's as fun as it is colorful. It's also genuinely hilarious. Plus you get to power-bomb your enemies . . .

GOAT SIMULATOR

It's a difficult one to recommend to gamers who want something that will keep them playing for a while, because they'll get bored with *Goat Simulator* within minutes—but it's a hoot. Play as a goat, jump around, lick people. Of course!

RETRO ROUNDUP

There are thousands of great retro games, but having to either hunt down or dust off an old console is never particularly easy. Thankfully, many publishers these days are remastering their classics, allowing us to play them on our Xbox Ones and PlayStation 4s.

While plenty more will head our way soon, we've already had lots return to date, such as *DuckTales: Remastered*, *The Sly Collection*, *The Legend of Zelda: The Wind Waker HD*, *Jak and Daxter Collection*, *Ratchet & Clank Collection*, *Capcom Classics Collection*, and *Sega Mega Drive Ultimate Collection*—the latter two containing a tremendous number of timeless gems that you both deserve and need to play. Make sure you hunt some of these down, and have yourself some fun with the gaming treasures of years past!

STATS

2001:
the year in which *Jak and Daxter* first debuted

52 million
copies of the *Zelda* franchise have been sold the world over

1
Scrooge McDuck in *DuckTales: Remastered*

22
titles can be played on *Capcom Classics Collection*

TOP **5** BEST RERELEASES

SUPER MARIO BROS.

1 Available through Nintendo's eShop, *Super Mario Bros.* is one of the most important video games in history. The second outing for Mario—who debuted in *Donkey Kong* as "Jumpman"— it's a definite classic.

SONIC THE HEDGEHOG

2 He's Sega's most famous creation and a character who's been around for over 20 years, and now you can play his original game again thanks to the *Sega Mega Drive Ultimate Collection*, available on Xbox 360 and PS3.

THE LEGEND OF ZELDA: THE WIND WAKER HD

3 Rereleased for Wii U in 2014, *The Wind Waker* is one of the best games in the *Zelda* series, and still great fun to play today.

STREET FIGHTER II: THE WORLD WARRIOR

4 You can play *Street Fighter II* in HD thanks to *Capcom Classics Collection* or through download on Xbox Live and PSN.

THE SLY COLLECTION

5 Sly Cooper always had a great following, and his original trilogy of games—*Sly Cooper and the Thievius Raccoonus*, *Sly 2: Band of Thieves*, and *Sly 3: Honor Among Thieves*—can now be played on your PlayStation 3.

DID YOU KNOW?

Talon and Ingo, two characters from the *Legend of Zelda* series, were based on the famous Nintendo pairing that is Mario and Luigi.

TIME LINE

2005 –	CAPCOM CLASSICS COLLECTION
2008 –	NAMCO MUSEUM: VIRTUAL ARCADE
2009 –	KONAMI CLASSICS VOLUME 1/2
2009 –	SEGA MEGA DRIVE ULTIMATE COLLECTION
2010 –	THE SLY COLLECTION
2011 –	DREAMCAST COLLECTION
2012 –	JAK AND DAXTER COLLECTION
2012 –	RATCHET & CLANK COLLECTION
2013 –	DUCKTALES: REMASTERED
2013 –	THE LEGEND OF ZELDA: THE WIND WAKER HD

ALSO CHECK OUT . . .

PAC-MAN: CE
This is a brilliant update of a retro classic, adding a combo system to the traditional Pac-Man vs. ghosts gameplay. Amazing graphics, too!

BEYOND GOOD & EVIL
The great *Beyond Good & Evil* was rereleased in HD for digital download in 2011.

THE SECRET OF MONKEY ISLAND
Point-and-click games are few and far between nowadays, so *The Secret of Monkey Island* is worth a look.

THE BEST HARDWARE

ATARI 2600

WHY: The Atari 2600 came out way back in 1977, and because it was made by the biggest gaming company at the time, it had all the biggest games like *Space Invaders*, *Asteroids*, and *Pac-Man*. It wasn't the first console, or even the first "modern" console, but it was the one that turned gaming into big business, and most of the other consoles here wouldn't exist without the Atari. It also hung around forever—because of its popularity, it was officially supported until 1992!

NINTENDO DS

WHY: The Nintendo DS is the bestselling handheld of all time. With 154 million sold since 2004, the original Nintendo DS was a monster based on the fact that the brilliantly simple touch-screen controls allowed players of all ages to pick it up easily. As a result of this wide appeal, Nintendo was selling games to everyone who would have them—*Dr. Kawashima's Brain Training* for your grandparents, the old-school *New Super Mario Bros.* for your parents, and *Pokémon* for you.

XBOX 360

WHY: It ushered in gaming's HD era. While Microsoft got its foot in the door of the console race with the original Xbox, it was 2005's Xbox 360 that made the American company into a major player. It was the first console for which all games had to support HD TV sets, and it helped popularize online gaming and downloadable games by including Xbox Live as standard—it's hard to imagine life without them now!

MEGA DRIVE

WHY: Sega's new Mega Drive console was more powerful than the NES, so Sega decided to go after Nintendo with ads that said its console could do "what Nintendon't"—and the arrival of the superfast *Sonic the Hedgehog* backed that up. Nintendo battled back with the SNES, and playground arguments raged for years. The Mega Drive was also home to *FIFA International Soccer*, the first game in the series, released way back in 1993.

GAME BOY

WHY: On paper, the Game Boy looked outmatched against the Sega Game Gear and Atari Lynx—those could show games in color and were more powerful. But the Game Boy was cheaper, and the black-and-white screen extended battery life, saving players a fortune in AAs. Having *Tetris* and *Pokémon*, some of the most popular games ever made, certainly didn't do any harm.

NINTENDO WII

WHY: Having been successful with the simple touch-screen controls of the DS, Nintendo kept it simple for the Wii with a motion-controlled remote that makes game control exactly what you expect. If you want to steer a car, turn the controller like a wheel; if you want to hit a tennis ball, take a swing. Nintendo made strong games like *Wii Sports* to show this off.

DID YOU KNOW?

The very first console was the Magnavox Odyssey, way back in 1972. It displayed only black-and-white graphics and couldn't play sounds!

COMMODORE 64

WHY: It's the most popular computer ever made. If you've ever heard your dad talking about waiting forever to load games from tape, he might have had a Commodore 64. Parents bought it because they thought it would help with homework, but kids were more interested in the games. You could also program your own games on it, creating a wave of "bedroom coders"—people making their own indie games.

NINTENDO ENTERTAINMENT SYSTEM

WHY: When the NES arrived in the United States in 1985, most shops didn't want to stock consoles, because they thought of gaming as a fad that was already over—players had lost interest in older consoles since the shelves were full of bad games. Nintendo's quality guarantee, as well as great games like *Super Mario Bros.* and *The Legend of Zelda*, allowed players to trust the people making their games again.

PLAYSTATION

WHY: Sony's arrival in the console market happened as games were shifting from cartridge to CD, and from 2-D to 3-D. The PlayStation had great-looking versions of big arcade hits like *Ridge Racer* as well as epic original games like *Final Fantasy VII*, which made it hugely popular. The console was the first to sell over 100 million units, a huge milestone that showed that gaming had become an everyday activity across the world.

PLAYSTATION 2

WHY: It's the bestselling console of all time. The PlayStation 2 was one of gaming's truly great machines. Everyone was making games for it after Sony did so well with the original PlayStation, so the PlayStation 2 had a game for you no matter what you enjoyed, from party games like *Guitar Hero* and *Singstar* to serious racing games like *Gran Turismo 4*. A staggering 155 million PlayStation 2 consoles were sold during the machine's lengthy 13-year lifespan!

THE EXPERT SAYS . . .

HOLLIE BENNETT
"PlayStationAccess" on YouTube

PLAYSTATION

My favorite console of all time is the original PlayStation; while so many others have delivered incredible gaming experiences, it still remains the one that I have the strongest emotional ties to. Growing up, I had always been lucky enough to own consoles, but when I was just a young kid playing games, it was *Final Fantasy VIII* that lit that fire within me, and my passion for gaming really started. Even now, 15 years later, I still think about those games I played every single day. The original PlayStation is the experience that my friends and I shared, and it's the fuel for nostalgic conversation that lasts until the early hours of the morning.

TOP 10 BEST FINAL LEVELS

GOLDENEYE 007

WHY: *GoldenEye* on the Nintendo 64 proved that a first-person shooter could work on a console. Its great final level, Cradle, ensured that there were barely any flaws from start to finish. A genuine shoot fest, it ended as you finally did away with boss Trevelyan before jumping onto a helicopter in flight.

BRAID

WHY: Most games put you in the shoes of the good guy. Why wouldn't they? We all want to be the hero. With *Braid*, though, this idea was turned on its head. The game allowed you to turn back time whenever you saw fit, and doing so after the last level showed that instead of being the white knight, you were the bad guy all along.

HALO 3

WHY: The *Halo* series has plenty of memorable levels, but few games have ended as well as *Halo 3*. With the world slowly falling to smithereens, players are told to jump in their Warthogs and floor them to safety. The game doesn't let up, from the moment they jump in the vehicles until they arrive at their destination.

GUITAR HERO 2

WHY: *Guitar Hero* is all about improving your skill. Even if you've played it for over 100 hours, though, you're still in for quite the challenge when you're asked to get through Lynyrd Skynyrd's "Free Bird." Lasting almost ten minutes, with a solo that would test even the best players, it's a great end.

REZ

WHY: It takes a lot to stand out in a game that's already as wonderfully different as *Rez*, but Area 5, the last level of the game, manages it. It constantly switches visual styles, and the last boss speaks to you as you fly through the stage, talking about life on Earth as the enemies twist and morph to match what she's saying!

SONIC THE HEDGEHOG 2

WHY: When you finally get to its last zone, *Sonic the Hedgehog 2* raises the bar. You come face-to-face with Metal Sonic. If you get past him somehow, it's straight on to Dr. Robotnik . . . who's constructed himself a huge mechanical suit!

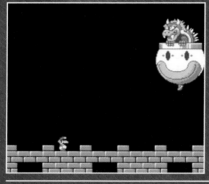

SUPER MARIO KART

WHY: *Super Mario Kart* has an incredible number of amazing tracks that have been getting better and better ever since its debut in 1992. Without a shadow of a doubt, though, the best course to finish one of its many cups came in the original game—Rainbow Road. Set in space and eliminating the barriers that so often kept you safe, the course sent you careering right off the concrete with only one wrong move.

SUPER MARIO WORLD

WHY: It would be hard to find someone who doesn't like *Super Mario World*, and its amazing last level just proves that the love is justified. Incorporating everything that made the game so good in the first place, the final Bowser's Castle asks so much of you that there's a huge sense of satisfaction when you pull it off. You feel like a platforming king! Throw in the intense final boss fight with Bowser himself, and it's one of the best in history.

THE LEGEND OF ZELDA: OCARINA OF TIME

WHY: One of the first things you see in *Ocarina of Time* is Hyrule Castle. Then Ganon reigns supreme and takes the landmark as his own. What once was a tower of peace is now a dungeon. It's also a structure you have to climb as the game comes to a close. It ends when you go head-to-head with Ganon himself.

SHADOW OF THE COLOSSUS

WHY: Every Colossi fight in *Shadow of the Colossus* is a giant puzzle, none more so than the last monster. Easily the biggest of the bunch, it asks you to figure out how to get to the beast's head without being knocked down to the ground. In reality, this is a platforming section that harks back to the likes of *Mario*. You'll need similar skills, too.

THE EXPERT SAYS . . .
JOSHUA MATTHEWS
"GamingFTL" on YouTube

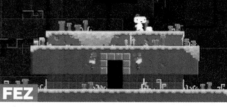

FEZ

 The final sequence of *FEZ* really stuck in my head. You get two different endings, depending on how much of it you complete, but I always preferred the non-100-percent one. A beautiful electronic version of Chopin's Prelude in E Minor plays as the world slowly degrades and pixelates in front of you. *Nidhogg*'s ending is always funny because the winner gets eaten by a giant worm! Then there are games I really loved playing and finishing when I was younger. *Wind Waker*'s final battle against Ganon was hard for me then. Completing its quest is something I'll always remember.

SHOVEL KNIGHT

SHOVEL KNIGHT

HARD-CORE PIXEL ACTION

Platforming games were notoriously difficult back in the NES days. Don't feel like you've missed out, though, since *Shovel Knight* is a throwback to those times, combining difficulty with smart level design and lovely pixel-art visuals.

MASTER GAMING JARGON

ADS

Aim Down Sights. This is often seen in first-person shooter games like *Call of Duty* and *Battlefield. Halo* famously did not have an ADS option until recently.

AFK

Away From Keyboard. This is usually a quick message to tell others that you won't be playing for a few minutes, to prevent them from kicking you out due to inactivity.

AGGRO

This term used to refer to any MMO creature that would attack you on sight, but now it means being attacked. If you "have aggro," for example, the creature is targeting you over the other players because you did a certain amount of damage to it.

AOE

Area Of Effect. This is a spell or ability that covers a wide area on the map rather than a specific target.

BOOSTING

When a group of players come together online to play in a specific way to bolster their leaderboard positions or unlock achievements. For example, they might set up an online game to kill one another over and over again.

CARRY

In MOBAs, a character that has to be "carried" by the team by farming items and gaining levels until late in the game, when their abilities will help dominate the opposition.

CHRISTMAS NOOB

One of the influx of new players in online multiplayers after Christmas.

This deluge is due to the large number of players who received new consoles or games as gifts.

CLUTCH
Used to describe a successful play at a critical moment in competitive gaming, usually determining the outcome of the game.

COUNTER
When a character, unit, or strategy dominates another character, unit, or strategy. Hard counter means the dominance is overwhelming, and soft counter means there's only a slight advantage in play.

CROSS-UP
IN A FIGHTING GAME, AN ATTACK THAT HAS TO BE BLOCKED FROM THE DIRECTION OPPOSITE TO HOW IT APPEARS. THIS MOST COMMONLY OCCURS WITH JUMPING ATTACKS AIMED AT THE OPPONENT'S HEAD.

DOUBLE ELIMINATION
The preferred tournament format for competitive gaming. This takes the form of a knockout tournament in which losing players are sent to a losers' bracket, where another knockout tournament is taking place. A player has to lose twice to be completely eliminated from the tournament—hence the name double elimination.

ENDGAME
The final stages of a game—for instance, in MOBAs when most champions have leveled up.

F2P
Free To Play.

GANKING
Most commonly used in MOBAs or MMORPGs to denote an "unfair fight" in which a player has a significant advantage over the target. This can be because the player is a higher level or is part of a group, because the target is low on health, or for other reasons.

GGWP
Good Game Well Played. The opposite is BG—Bad Game.

GRIEFING
When players annoy or harass other players by using game mechanics in unintended ways. For example, this could include aggroing monsters toward players not prepared to fight them, trapping teammates by standing in their way, kill stealing, and so on.

GRINDING
Doing repetitive tasks, such as killing monsters, over and over again in order to level up characters or abilities and make the game easier.

HARD BAN
When certain aspects of a game, such as stages or characters, have been banned from competitive play.

HIGH-LEVEL
Refers to the competitive level of play between experts who have figured out the most effective strategies and tactics.

KITING
In an MMORPG, kiting is grabbing a mob's attention and then walking away so as to guide it in a certain direction. In a MOBA, kiting is attacking from a distance so that the opponent can't easily attack back.

L2P
LEARN TO PLAY. THIS IS OFTEN SHOUTED AT NOOBS.

LAG TACTICS
Strategies that are more effective in games in which there is significant lag and are frowned upon because they would otherwise be ineffective.

MASTER GAMING JARGON

LUCKSACK
A derogatory term for a player who wins because of good luck, despite poor play overall.

METAGAME
Refers to a certain game's current play style, as determined by trends in competitive play as new tactics are discovered and the balance is tweaked.

MIA
Missing In Action. This term originated in *League of Legends* and means that an opponent has disappeared from their "lane" and could therefore pose a danger to the rest of the team.

MIND GAME
Any tactic in competitive gaming that works primarily on a psychological level—that is, it messes with your opponent's mind. For example, you might taunt someone in *Street Fighter* and then attack immediately following the taunt, expecting your opponent to try to hit you out of the taunt to stop your mocking.

MOBA
Multiplayer Online Battle Arena. This is the genre of games that includes *League of Legends*, *DOTA 2*, and so on.

NO-SCOPING
Killing someone with a sniper rifle without "scoping." This is one of the hardest feats to pull off in a competitive shooter.

NOOB
A NEW GAMER. THE TERM STARTED AS *n00b*, WHICH ITSELF WAS A SHORTENED VERSION OF *NEWBIE*.

NPC
Non-Playable Character.

PERMADEATH
WHAT HAPPENS WHEN DEATH WIPES OUT ALL YOUR STATS AND PROGRESS, FORCING YOU TO START THE GAME OVER AGAIN.

PVE
Player Versus Environment. Most typically used in MMORPGs, this means players versus computer-controlled enemies rather than versus other players. Usually, PvE can be played alone and contains some sort of story line.

PVP
Player Versus Player. Most typically used in MMORPGs, this pits players against one another and, depending on the game, can be triggered by switching PvP mode on, by entering PvP zones, and so forth.

RAGEQUIT
When someone quits a game early, usually out of frustration at losing.

RE-SPEC
When you reset the stats on your character to build him or her in a different way.

ROGUE-LIKE
A genre of games that typically feature 2-D pixel graphics, permadeath, a high degree of difficulty, and randomly generated dungeons. These games are inspired by the 1980 game *Rogue*.

SALT
Term for when players take defeat poorly. This was shortened from *salty tears*.

SCRUB
A derogatory term for a player who is overconfident and boastful despite not being very skilled. A scrub is not necessarily the same as a noob, since a scrub may not be new to a game.

MASTER GAMING JARGON

SHERPA
An experienced player who helps noobs beat games. Most commonly seen in MMOs such as *Destiny*.

SMURFING
When highly skilled players create new accounts with lower rankings so that they are matched against lesser players online.

SOFT BAN
When certain aspects of a game, such as stages or characters, are frowned on in competitive play but official bans are not enforced.

SPAWN CAMPING
In team deathmatch, when one team pushes another back to its spawn point and then camps around that area, killing players as they spawn. Games will often have mechanics to prevent this from happening (spawn points that change, temporary invulnerability granted to spawning players, and so on).

TIER LIST
A ranking of characters in a competitive multiplayer game. A high-tier character is really good; a low-tier character lacks certain tools or moves necessary to compete. For example, in *Street Fighter IV*, Dan is considered a low-tier character.

TURTLE
An extremely defensive player.

VANILLA
Used to describe the original or base game, without any expansions, add-ons, or sometimes even patches present. For example, a vanilla server in *Minecraft* is one without modifications or expansions.

WHALE
A big spender on free-to-play games.

WHIFF
An attack that does no damage because it misses. Although this is usually accidental, some players deliberately whiff attacks for tactical reasons—for example, to build super meter in fighting games.

ZONING
IN FIGHTING GAMES, USING NORMAL AND SPECIAL MOVES TO KEEP OPPONENTS AT A VERY SPECIFIC DISTANCE AT WHICH YOUR OPTIONS ARE GREATER THAN THEIRS.

LIST OF GAMES

LIST OF GAMES

LIST OF GAMES

LIST OF GAMES

LIST OF GAMES